Unseen Treasures

Imperial Russia and the New World

A Millennium Exhibition from the Russian State Historical Museum

Organized by the American-Russian Cultural Cooperation Found
and the Russian State Historical Museum in commemoration
of the 200th anniversary of the creation of the Russian-American Company

The New Jersey State Museum, Trenton, NJ: December 1999–April 2000
The Missouri Historical Society, St. Louis, MO: May–August 2000
The Mint Museum of Art, Charlotte, NC: September–January 2001
The Presidio Trust Exhibition Hall, Presidio,
San Francisco, CA: March–June 2001

Institutions lending to the exhibition

Russian State Historical Museum, Moscow
State Archive of the Russian Federation
National Archives and Records Administration of the United States
The Alaska Department of Natural Resources
Collection of John C. Middleton

Cover: Portrait Badge with Alexander II and Alexander III

Title Page: Flag of the Russian-American Trading Company

Back cover: Deerskin vestments of an Orthodox priest

Inside front cover: Letter of Leo Tolstoy in English to the North American newspaper *Philadelphia* on his attitude toward the Russo-Japanese war; 1904-1905

Inside back cover: Letter of Thomas Jefferson to Jean Baptiste Say, a French economist; 1817

Designed by Graphic Design & Production in association with Virginia Lithograph

Printed by Virginia Lithograph, Arlington, Virginia

Published by the American-Russian Cultural Cooperation Foundation

©1999 American-Russian Cultural Cooperation Foundation and the Russian State Historical Museum, Moscow

Library of Congress Card Number: 99-068432

ISBN 0-9675441-0-6

Preface

Unseen Treasures: Imperial Russia and the New World, is a happy and timely reminder of a cordial and mutually beneficial relationship that has endured 200 years of the vicissitudes of history. Russia supported American independence in the reign of Catherine the Great and subsequently encouraged President Lincoln during his struggle to preserve our Union. These are but two examples of the 19th century bonds between our two countries.

A brisk trade developed between us; and a partnership with the nations of the Pacific began along the west coast of North America which soon engaged the infant industries of our young Republic from coast to coast. The hulls of Boston-based merchantmen carried much of the commerce. Today as we contemplate and implement the growing interdependence of business enterprises, we are here reminded that we are not so much preparing new ground as following furrows first ploughed by our pioneering ancestors in both countries. Their example - so vividly displayed in this extraordinary exhibit - is one that we should all be proud to follow.

James Billington
Librarian of Congress

Acknowledgements

The American-Russian Cultural Cooperation Foundation

Founded in 1992 by a group of distinguished Americans, the American-Russian Cultural Cooperation Foundation strives to encourage and support increased cultural exchanges between the United States and Russia. Recognizing that art and culture are important factors in American-Russian relations, and that knowledge and trust can be enhanced through cultural dialogue, the Foundation promotes, through its programs and cultural events, the advancement of social, political, business and economic relations between the two nations.

US Organizing Committee
  Chairman of the Board
    The Hon. James W. Symington

  Executive Director
    Alexander P. Potemkin

  Directors
    Dwayne O. Andreas
    Michael B. Goldstein
    Donald M. Kendall
    John Krimsky, Jr.
    Rabbi Arthur Schneier
    Shelley M. Zeiger

Russian Honorary Committee
  H.E. Yuri V. Ushakov
    Ambassador of the Russian Federation
  Vladimir K. Egorov
    Minister of Culture of the Russian Federation
  Vladimir P. Kozlov
    Chief of the Federal Archival Service
  Alexander I. Shkourko
    Director General of the State Historical Museum
  Sergei V. Mironenko
    Director of the State Archive of the Russian Federation
  Tamara G. Igoumnova
    Deputy Director General of the State Historical Museum

Concept and Structure of the Exhibition: N.A. Kargapolova, M.P. Swezey

Working Group: T. G. Igoumnova, N.A. Kargapolova, M.P. Swezey, S. Hoffman, O.V. Marinin, A.P. Potemkin

Curator: N.A. Kargapolova

Guest Curator: M. P. Swezey

Editor of the catalogue: M. P. Swezey

Authors of the Catalog annotations: T.S. Aleshina, M.A. Bubchikova, V.E. Bulatov, N.I . Vyshar, L.N. Goncharova, N.N. Goncharova, O.G. Gordeyeva, M.K. Gurenok, L.A. Dementieva, D.A. Dimentman, T.I. Dulkina, V.A. Durov, L.V. Efimova, E.Y. Elkova, I.P. Erokhina, A.K. Zaitsev, E.I. Itkina, L.A. Kornukova, P.A. Koshelev, E.D. Markina, O.N. Melnikova, N.G. Meniaylo, O.V. Molchanova, I.N. Paltusova, A.A. Petrov, L.A. Petrova, N.A. Perevezentseva, I.M. Pyrova, L.Y. Rudneva, M.V. Sidorova, I.A. Semakova, E.P. Smirnova, G.G. Smorodinova, E.I. Serebriakova, V.P. Solomentseva, N.N. Skorniakova, Y.E. Fagurel, T.V. Chistonogova, A.E. Khokhlov, I.S. Shikanova, A.D. Yanovsky

Photography: V.M. Boyko, M.N. Kravtsov, V.A. Mochugovsky, E.A. Rasdobarin, V.S. Glebov, Dennis Wyszynski, Willian C. Brumfield

Exhibition Designer: Jon Bentz

Designer for Graphic Objects: S.L. Teplov

Exhibition Fabrications: Explus, Inc.

Computer preparation of exhibition materials: N.G. Lukashova, N.M. Malutina, K.A. Meerov, L. Shaw, D. Ulman

Restorers: T. V. Avdusina, V. Alymov, I. P. Baigulova, K.B. Belianinov, V.E. Belanovsky, E.E. Vodzinskaya, A.V. Volkova, L.I. Vinogradova, E.Y. Guzeyeva, O.O. Dolganova, T.A. Zhabilina, Y.V. Zhuravsky, A.G. Kalinin, A.V. Kozlov, C.P. Koriakina, L.A. Kologrivova, O. B. Lantratova, Y.V. Matveyeva, S.A. Novikov, E.G. Perova, G.A. Peskova, A.D. Petrova, V.G. Pogodin, A.G. Riabinkov, A. Slanikov, A.A. Sidorov, A.I. Sidorov, I.B. Skrul, D.A. Sorokin, A.V. Stepnev, P.A. Turischeva, V.M. Shepilov, T.N. Yutanova

The American-Russian Cultural Cooperation Foundation wishes to acknowledge the invaluable support provided for the San Francisco venue by the Trust for Mutual Understanding.

The Foundation also would like to express its appreciation to the Hasenkamp Company for its excellent services and kind consideration.

Table of Contents

Preface   *iii*
James Billington

Introductory remarks   *vii*
    H. E. Yuri V. Ushakov,
        Ambassador of the Russian Federation
    Alexander I. Shkourko,
        Director of the State Historical Museum
    Alexander P. Potemkin,
        Executive Director of the ARCCF

Foreword   *xv*
    Nicholas N. Bolkhovitinov

Unseen Treasures: Imperial Russia and the New World   1
    Natalia A. Kargapolova

Forgotten Dreams, the Story of Rezanov and "Conchita"   13
    James W. Symington

Archaeology at Alaska's Castle Hill, the Colonial Capital of Russian America   17
    Dave McMahan

Daily Life in Colonial Russian America   23
    John C. Middleton

The Mission of St. Innokenty (Veniaminov) in Unalaska   29
    Marilyn P. Swezey

From Notes on the Islands of the Unalaska District   35
    Ivan Veniaminov

Color Illustrations and Annotations   41

Checklist of Objects   73

Biographical Index   95

Russian State Historical Museum, Moscow

The State Historical Museum is the largest museum of national history in Russia. Its collection numbers more than four million relics and 10 million pages of documents. In travelling around the holdings of the museum, one can cover five hundred thousand years in a single day, starting with the paleolithic and ending with the present day.

Alexander III opened the Historical Museum in 1883. As patrons of the museum, the Imperial Family visited the museum constantly, invited honored guests there and built up its collection.

The groundwork for everything the museum has now was laid a hundred years ago by two scholars. They laid the theoretical, scholarly foundation, developed the stylistic architectural concept for the building and the 48 halls and filled the museum depositories with objects and documents. They were very different: Count A. S. Uvarov (1858-1884), the owner of luxurious estates and palaces and possessor of splendid collections, an archeologist and the most learned man in Russia, and I. Ye. Zabelin (1820-1908), an orphan with a third-grade education from a school for orphans, a "brilliant Russian mind," a consummate expert on ancient times and the author of well-known books on the lives and times of the Russian tsars. Their goal was to create a museum in which historical materials would be gathered from every corner of the nation.

The enormous collections of the museum were accumulated due to the donations of individuals and organizations and purchases by the museum of monuments of history and art. Well-known Russian collectors, who collected unique objects all their lives and spent enormous amounts of money on them, later passed their treasures on to the museum. The personnel of the museum traditionally participate in archaeological digs and expeditions, which gives them the opportunity to add to the archaeological and ethnographic collections. There have been 350 archaeological and 200 ethnographic expeditions in the last 50 years. The holdings of the museum are divided into departments according to the types of materials. For example, there are departments for fabrics, precious metals, paintings, manuscripts, weapons, ceramics, etc. Due to the quantity and variety of the objects stored there, the Historical Museum could rightly be called an encyclopedia of Russian history and culture. In addition to collection departments, the museum has several scholarly departments that work on problems of the history of Russia. The museum is a great center of scholarship and publishes its own scholarly collection. Individual monographs and albums and popular scientific literature are published and lectures are given at the museum, study circles operate there, and there are trips for various segments of the general public. Special attention is devoted to school children and students. There were 600,000 visitors to the museum in 1998.

Remarkable relics of Russian history from the collection of the State Historical Museum have been exhibited in many countries of the world. The museum participates in the work of the Executive Committee of the International Council of Museums (of UNESCO) and its committees and symposia.

N. A. Kargapolova

State Archive of the Russian Federation

The State Archive of the Russian Federation (GARF) was established in 1992 as a result of the merging of the Central State Archive of the October Revolution, High State Government Bodies and State Administrative Agencies of the USSR (TsGAOR SSSR) and the Central State Archive of the RSFSR (TsGA RSFSR). GARF is the largest regularly growing repository of documents on the history of Russia, the USSR, the RSFSR and the Russian Federation, with more than 5 million files dating from 1800 to the present.

GARF includes about 1 million files on the history of pre-revolutionary Russia and more than 3 million files on the history of the RSFSR, the USSR and the RF.

The Archive in recent years has participated in more than 50 exhibitions. The partners of the Archive in the creation of large-scale historical and artistic exhibitions are such well-known museum repositories as the State Hermitage, the State Historical Museum, the Peterhof, Tsarskoye Selo and Pavlovsk museum preserves and the Museum of Private Collections, etc. The "Treasures of Russia," "Nicholas and Alexandra" and "Nicholas II. A Family Album" exhibits were submitted for the attention of the American public in 1996-1999, and there are agreements for the creation and exhibition in the United States of other exhibits which make use of the extremely rich archive holdings of GARF.

GARF is the largest scholarly publishing center of the Russian Federation.

M.V. Sidorova

AMBASSADOR
OF THE RUSSIAN FEDERATION
TO THE USA

M E S S A G E
of the Ambassador of the Russian Federation to the USA
Yuri V. Ushakov
to participants and visitors of the exhibition

"IMPERIAL RUSSIA AND THE NEW WORLD"

August " 2 ", 1999

This exhibition is in celebration of a memorable event in the history of Russian-American relations - the 200th anniversary of the creation of the Russian-American Company. The Company's early activities in Alaska and Northern California established the basis for mutually beneficial trade as well as economic and cultural contacts between the two countries. Russians and Americans have always shared a pioneering spirit, and we are proud of our ancestors' initiatives in the discovery and settlement of North America as well as their support for the independence of the young American nation.

I am sure each visitor will find something of special interest in this first-time display of extraordinary historic treasures.

May this exhibition reinforce the long-standing ties between our two nations as we approach the new Millennium.

My very best wishes to you all.

Yuri V.Ushakov

The State Historical Museum accepted with enthusiasm a proposal of the American-Russian Cultural Cooperation Foundation to mark the 200th Anniversary of the Russian-American Company by organizing the exhibition *Unseen Treasures: Imperial Russia and the New World* in a number of U.S. cities.

During its 125 years of existence the State Historical Museum has acquired an enormous collection on the history, culture and art of Russia, consisting of 4.5 million artifacts. Together with the State Archive of the Russian Federation we are presenting at this exhibition more than 300 objects. We trust that visitors will become acquainted with the revealing pages of the 200-years history of relations between Russia and the United States. Visitors will see for the first time the unfolding story of Russia's efforts to enter world oceans and its contributions to the early development of the North American Territory. This exhibition conveys the unique traditions of the Russian people at the dawn of diplomatic and economic relations between our states.

I would like to believe that in this last year of the Millennium our exhibition will acquaint American viewers with pivotal moments in the 200-year relationship between our two countries, and in that way contribute to mutual understanding and cooperation.

Alexander I. Shkourko
Director General of the State Historical Museum

The American-Russian Cultural Cooperation Foundation is proud to present to the American public the exhibition *Unseen Treasures: Imperial Russia and the New World*. The essential component of the Foundation's activity has been commemorative programs devoted to the common historical heritage of both nations, such as special events, exhibitions, and concerts. The Foundation has celebrated the 200th anniversary of the Russian Orthodox Church in America, the contribution of the Russian settlers in Northern California, the 125th anniversary of Russian Grand Duke Alexis's Goodwill Mission to the United States, the 50th anniversary of joint victory in World War II and the historic Elbe-river meeting of Russian and American soldiers. It has also honored such distinguished contemporary contributors to that heritage as Mstislav Rostropovich, Van Cliburn and Igor Moiseyev.

By this exhibition we wish to remind Americans as well as Russians of the early Russian explorations and activities in what was then called Russian America. We wish to demonstrate that this was a long and meaningful period in the history of both nations as they interacted with imagination and mutual benefit. It was a time when Alaska and part of Northern California were settled by pioneers, both Russian and then American. Therefore, this vast land has, so to speak, two parents. It is our hope that the memory of the Russian American realm will not be submerged beneath our joint consciousness as if it were Russian Atlantis. I hope that visitors to this exhibition will feel with reverence the silent presence of Peter the Great and William Penn, Catherine the Great and Benjamin Franklin, Alexander II and President Lincoln as well as many other of our respective forefathers.

I would like to use this opportunity to thank the Russian State Historical Museum and the State Archive of the Russian Federation, which diligently preserve the precious objects representing the historic and cultural legacy of both nations, for sharing their precious artifacts with us. Especially I thank their directors Alexander Shkourko and Sergei Mironenko for their trust in providing these treasures for the exhibition in the United States. Finally, my deep appreciation goes to the Russians Tamara Igoumnova and Natalia Kargapolova as well as the American, Marilyn Swezey for their diligent and creative curatorial efforts to mold and organize this exhibit; indeed, to all Russian and American participants who contributed so generously to this historical enterprise.

Alexander P. Potemkin
Executive Director

Foreword

July 8/19, 1999 marks two hundred years from the date of the founding of the famous Russian-American Company (RAC), which managed the property of Russia in the far northwest region of America until 1867.

There is no question that the formation of the RAC marked the beginning of a new stage in the history of Russian colonization of the Northwest in America, and the very existence of the company and its activities were governed by the appropriate "privileges" and "regulations."

It is customary to think of the Russian colonization of the Aleutian Islands and Alaska as a direct continuation of the colonization of Siberia and the concluding stage in the process of the eastward expansion of Russia over many centuries. The view of historians normally has covered the common features of the conquest of Siberia and Russian America, and only much more rarely have researchers devoted any attention to the differences. However, there were also differences; moreover, these differences seem quite substantial.

The main and defining feature of the Russian colonization of the American Northwest lies in the fact that it was of a maritime nature and in this regard differed fundamentally from the colonization of Siberia, which was of a pronounced continental nature. It is just this characteristic which defined the basic features of the conquest of Russian America and, in the final analysis, its sad fate.

The seagoing fleet (primarily the Navy), although it began to play an important role in the foreign policy of Russia in the time of Peter I, was never a main factor in foreign policy. Even during the years of the height of the Russian Empire - in the period of the victory over Napoleon I - the army continued to be the main force. The Crimean War of 1853-1856 served as a graphic demonstration that Russia was unable to stand against strong naval powers on the sea. It is not by chance that the plans to sell Russian America to the United States emerged at just this time.

The difference between the seagoing colonization of Russian America and the continental colonization of Siberia literally can be defined in two words: the sable and the kalan (sea otter). The Russians were led to the endless expanse of Siberia by the "sable" and the valuable fur of the "sea beaver" beckoned them to the shores of Russian America. Siberian furs (sable, ermine and squirrel, among others) went to the European markets – to Moscow and Leipzig and later to St. Petersburg, as well as to Holland and England - where they were exchanged for various metal products, fabrics, colonial goods, etc. Sea otters, on the other hand, were especially prized in China. They were imported into China and exchanged there for tea, silk, porcelain and other Chinese goods. To a certain extent, one can say – as Professor J. Gibson has concluded – that the fur of the sea otter, which was so highly prized by the Chinese aristocracy, promoted to a great extent the development of the Russian tradition of drinking tea and at the same time strengthened business connections with China.

A perceptive Canadian researcher has also devoted attention to a number of differences in the colonization of Siberia and Alaska. In Siberia, for example, work on the sable industry took place mainly during the winter, which left enough time to work in agriculture during the summer.

It is not surprising, therefore, that most of the population of Siberia has been working in the field of agriculture, especially field crops, for a long time. The hardy strains of Siberian wheat aroused interest even on the part of American scientists as early as the 18th century. The sea otter and sealskin trade in Russian America began in the spring and lasted all summer, which naturally prevented agricultural work.

The fur trade, and the trade in marine animals, in particular, was carried on quite successfully at the end of the 18th century and during the early decades of the 19th century. The endeavors brought in significant revenues for the RAC. Between 1797 – 1821, for example, according to data from P. A. Turkmenev, sea otters, fur seals, beaver tails, otters, river beavers and other furs totaling 16,370,695 rubles 95 kopecks were exported from the colonies.

The merchants Shelikhov and Golikov were putting forward plans to expand the influence of Russia in the Pacific, but they were not able to enlist the support of the government. Plans for the expansion of the Ross colony also failed to receive support from the government; the fate of the colony was uncertain from the very beginning. For almost the entire 19th century (up to the sale of Alaska in 1867), the number of Russians held at a level of 400 – 800 (the peak was 823 in 1839). A comparatively insignificant part of the Russian population worked in the hunting and fur trade (most of the work fell to the local population, especially the Eskimos, Coniagmiutes and Aleuts). According to S. G. Fedorova, "80% of the Russian population was involved in the fields of management, technical maintenance of the trading fleet and defense of the colonies."

Although experiments for the development of livestock breeding were conducted quite successfully in the colonies, with swine and sheep multiplying especially rapidly, the Russians taught the natives to grow vegetables as well, especially potatoes. Only a very slight segment of the population was engaged in agriculture in Russian America (with the exception, perhaps, of the Ross colony).

It was extremely expensive to deliver food supplies and other goods by way of Siberia. Setting up round-the-world voyages from St. Petersburg to Russian America also failed to solve the problem. Trading with the "Boston ship men" and through intermediaries, with the Hudson Bay Company, California and the Hawaiian Islands proved more successful. At the same time, competition from foreign countries was growing stronger: first Spain and then England, and by the end of the 18th century, the United States, which later began to dominate the entire northern Pacific region. In the final analysis, Russia was not able to solidify its supremacy in the extreme northwest region of North America, and the power of the RAC in fact never extended over the entire population of continental Alaska.

At the same time, there were many positive results of the activities of the RAC in Alaska - numerous geographic discoveries, ethnographic research, the organization of school-based education and the founding of hospitals and libraries, not to mention shipbuilding and the development of various trades. In particular, Russian seamen were able to study in detail the coast of Alaska and other areas of the North Pacific, including the Russian Far East, Sakhalin and the Kurile Islands. Land expeditions of the RAC (I. Ya. Vasilyev, F. L. Kolmakov, A. K. Glazunov and L. A. Zagoskin, among others) which covered territories far into northern Alaska also made an important contribution to the development of geographic knowledge. The first hospitals, libraries and schools, which were intended to serve not only the Russians but also other residents of the RAC colonies (Aleuts, Creoles and Glinkites) as well, brought approval and admiration of contemporaries, including foreigners.

An important contribution of the Russians in Alaska is associated with the activities of the Orthodox Church, which became the protector of the local population from the very beginning. It is not by chance that the monk Herman, a member of the first ecclesiastical mission to Alaska, who became the first Orthodox saint in the Western Hemisphere, and, in particular, Innokentiy (I. Veniaminov), whose selfless work continues to arouse general admiration, are both still remembered and revered in Alaska. He is also a canonized saint.

On the whole, the differences between the continental colonization of Siberia and the maritime colonization of Russian American in the end determined their fate: Siberia became an integral part of Russia, and Russian America in 1867 passed into the possession of the United States.

N. N. Bolkhovitinov

Nikolai Bolkhovitinov is a senior scientific staff member of the Russian Academy of Sciences and a professor of American History at Moscow State University

Above: Parade on Palace Square in St. Petersburg, A.I. Ladurner and E.D. Tiedmann, 1855
Opposite: Portrait Badge with Alexander II and Alexander III

Unseen Treasures: Imperial Russia and the New World

Natalia A. Kargapolova

Jubilees in the lives of people and of states present a good opportunity to remember the past and to think about the future. The 200th anniversary of the founding of the Russian-American Company is an opportune occasion for a journey from Russia to America and to learn more about the history of our relationship.

A traveler heading for the New World in the 19th century from the brilliant, capital city of St. Petersburg, would travel across the Urals, through vast spaces in Siberia, cross the Bering Straits and the ocean to North America. Finally he would return to Russia and to Moscow, one of its most ancient cities. During his trip he will visit the study of Peter the Great, glimpse the ambiance of Catherine the Great, visit a Siberian house, sail aboard a Russian ship, attend an Orthodox church service and be present at the coronation of Alexander II in Moscow. The traveler will learn that the two countries are linked through the activities of emperors, the aristocracy, merchants, businessmen, writers, diplomats, sailors and travelers.

The journey begins in St. Petersburg, the city of Peter the Great's vision. As founder of the Russian fleet, he was focused on the future and turned his attention to North America perhaps in some way influenced by his conversation with William Penn in London in 1698. Peter received many requests from Dutch and French scholars who were curious to know whether Eurasia and North America were joined by land. At that time Russia was an enormous country, located both in Europe and Asia, with a population of more than 20 million people. Still in shock after the many reforms introduced by Peter the Great, Russia was continuously moving forward politically and economically as well as expanding its geographical periphery. On orders from Peter, the naval expedition of Vitus Bering was sent out. Commencing in 1728, it was unprecedented in its duration and the number of participants (up to 5000 people). After many complicated ordeals and hardships, Bering's second Kamchatka expedition traveling on the ships *St. Peter* and *St. Paul*, reached the North American coast on July 15 and 16, 1741. This was the beginning of the Russian exploration of the land that was later named Russian-America, and blazed the trail for numerous hunting and fishing expeditions and trading companies in the latter half of the 18th century.

Drawings and prints of the 18th and 19th centuries depict the stateliness of one of the most beautiful cities in the world built by the will of the Emperor on impassable swamps (in 2003 St. Petersburg will be celebrating its 300th anniversary). In a small silver box is kept a precious medal commemorating the Treaty of Nystad with Sweden in 1721, one of the most important events of Peter's rule. By this treaty Russia acquired an entry to the Baltic Sea and passage to the world's oceans.

A glass beaker, that can be seen in the exhibition, was made in the factory of A. Menshikov, Peter's friend and companion who was taken into state service not on his knowledge of manufacturing but on his personal human qualities. Menshikov rose from obscurity to a brilliant career. He became one of the most important statesmen in the country and was given the title of Prince. On the products made at his factory, he would sometimes place inscriptions glorifying Peter, as can be seen on the glass beaker. Peter liked to honor enterprising merchants and traders as can be seen on the silver kovsh awarded to the merchant Elyseev. Such a gift was a traditional award for services to the country at that time. Painted wall panels with moralistic and symbolic subjects were very much in the spirit and fashion of Peter's age and usually adorned the walls and doors of a drawing room or study, as seen in the first gallery of the exhibition.

Russia has always valued the role of Peter I in the country's history and this Emperor is featured in many works of art. Take for instance, the magnificent silver sculpture *Peter I on his Botik*, that was made to commemorate the 200th anniversary of the Russian navy. The Emperor is portrayed standing on the deck of his first small boat, *The Grandfather of the Russian Navy*. He is surrounded by all the regalia of his state power and enjoying the peak of his glory as a social reformer.

From Peter's study we move to the domain of a remarkable woman. Foreign by origin, she understood very well the problems of Russia and became an inalienable part of Russian life. Her people not only added the word "Great" to her name, but also Mother. It was during her reign (1762-1796) that the foundation

Fig. 1.
Peter I by an unknown artist from the original
by I.N. Nikitin
oil on canvas
Second half of the 18th century
State Historical Museum, Moscow

Fig. 2.
Catherine II by K. L.I. Khristinek
from the original by F.S. Rokotov
1780
oil on canvas
State Historical Museum, Moscow

for political relations between Russia and the United States were laid. From the very beginning of the American War for Independence, Russia maintained a policy of neutrality. On September 1, 1775 George III sent a personal letter to Catherine II, requesting that she send Russian soldiers to "suppress the uprising in the American colonies". The British Ambassador in St. Petersburg added a request to send 20,000 troops. In his letter to a member of Parliament he wrote that Russian soldiers would be "charming guests in New York" and "would civilize beautifully" that part of America. On September 23, Catherine politely but decisively refused. "I am just beginning to enjoy peace and my empire requires tranquility". Russia's political interests had always guided Catherine II and she was capable of evaluating international situations without any bias. In his turn, Washington wrote the following concerning the Russian position. "We were more than a little joyful to learn from a reliable source that the requests and proposals of the British to the Russian Empress have been rejected with contempt" and that "the Russian government has demonstrated respect for human rights" (from a letter to Lafayette). In 1780 the Russian government drafted a "Declaration of Armed Neutrality at Sea" that was supported by a majority of European countries. This declaration discouraged England from attempts to blockade American shores and made possible the victory of those fighting for independence. Many Russian aristocrats sympathized with the Americans, including A.A. Bezborodko, the Empress' powerful secretary, E.P. Dashkova, President of the St. Petersburg Academy of Sciences, and others. Benjamin Franklin's book *Poor Richard's Almanac* was very popular in Russia. Biographies of Washington, Franklin, Lafayette and Jefferson were published in Russia. In 1793-1796 the seafarer Y.F. Lisiansky, visited many cities of the young republic and spoke highly of Franklin

and Washington. Russian scholars, statesmen and explorers joined the American Philosophical Society founded by Franklin "for the furthering of useful knowledge." In his speech at the Jubilee session of the Society, Dr. Thomas Bond, vice-president, stressed that "Russia is rising to a brilliant future. She started searching for great scientists all over the world and encourages all the genres of literature in every possible way. There is something in common between Russia and America. . . Science finds itself in the care of a common friendship and does not know animosity or hostility."

The Empress herself became very interested in scientific ties with America. Catherine was busy working on the preparation of a comparative dictionary of all of the languages in the world. She wrote about it to Lafayette and asked him to send her a dictionary of American Indian words. The materials were sent to St. Petersburg and with it came an expression of good wishes from Washington to the Empress. "The discovery of linguistic unity is a step toward the development of unity between peoples," he wrote.

The superb portraits of Catherine are enhanced by portraits of some of the most celebrated people in Russia who contributed greatly to the development of friendly relations between the two countries. The striking carnival sleigh "Minerva" testifies to the magnificent ceremonial pageant masterminded by the young Empress for her coronation festivities. Russians had never seen anything like it: a procession of 200 carriages and sleighs moving majestically and accompanied by loud music. In each one was a person representing symbolically one of the human vices, while Minerva (the Roman goddess of Wisdom whom Catherine personified) punished them, sowing seeds of goodness and enlightenment. F. Volkov, the founder of the Russian theatre, wrote the script for the pageant.

Catherine's white kid gloves also have their own story to tell, connected with the first orphanage in Russia. Abandoned babies and babies born out of wedlock were brought to the orphanage from all over the country. They were brought up and given an education. The Empress took the orphanage under her special patronage. Once when she was visiting the orphanage someone asked for her gloves and she left them as a souvenir. The gold markers in the exhibition reveal her partiality for gambling. Catherine's personal taste can be discerned by the things that she liked, such as the objects made of steel using the technique of diamond cutting, a specialty of the armaments factory established by Peter the Great in Tula, not far from Moscow. The secret of this technique was known only in England and Tula.

The grandsons of Catherine, Emperors Alexander I and Nicholas I continued her foreign policy and during the reign of Alexander I Russia established diplomatic relations with the United States. An official border of the Russian colonies in North America was established and a convention was signed "preserving a durable relationship between the two powers".

Alexander I had a personal correspondence with President Jefferson in which their common interests were underlined. Jefferson sent to Alexander I as his personal gifts a 4 volume *Life of George Washington* and a copy of the Constitution of the United States. A bust of Alexander I was sent to Jefferson which was kept in his study at Monticello. The first Russian Minister to the United States, F.D. Pahlen, visited Jefferson at Monticello in the spring of 1811. Writing to the Foreign Minister, Rumiantsev, he described "Mr. Jefferson" as a man who "combines the rare qualities of statesman, scholar and likable man. He always speaks of his attachment to His Majesty with the greatest warmth," he continued,

Fig. 3.
Silver and enamel case for eyeglasses of Catherine II and her gold game markers, late 18th Century. State Historical Museum, Moscow

and "appreciates the rare qualities of the philanthropic sovereign whose bust is found in his study". After the victory over Napoleon, Russia gained the respect of many countries of the world. The United States had an occasion to seek the mediation of the Russian government at the time of the Napoleonic Wars when Danish authorities put a lien on numerous American ships. Adams, the American envoy to St. Petersburg, turned to Alexander I protesting the unlawful measures of the Danish authorities. The Emperor recommended to the Danish government that it hasten its investigation and return the American possessions as soon as possible. Denmark could do nothing but agree. St. Petersburg society was talking for quite some time about the conversation between Alexander I and W. Pinckney, the American Ambassador, at a magnificent New Year's reception that took place in the Winter Palace attended by 18,000 guests.

When looking for someone to assign as ambassador to Russia during the reign of

Fig. 4.
Alexander I by George Dawe, 1825, oil on canvas
State Historical Museum, Moscow

Fig. 5.
A Siberian Merchant's Wife
by an unknown artist
circa 1800
oil on canvas.
State Historical Museum, Moscow

Nicholas I, President Jackson wrote to John Randolph, a Virginian, that he would "like very much for this job to be assigned to one of the most gifted and distinguished of our countrymen." In the course of his diplomatic mission, Randolph mentioned the courtesy of the Russian authorities. "Nicholas I is the first Monarch in Europe and a true gentleman, and the Empress a true First Lady," he said. On December 18, 1832 during the reign of Nicholas I, Russia and the United States signed the first trade agreement regulating commerce and business relations between the two countries. On the initiative of the American envoy, Buchanan planned the signing of the agreement for the names-day of Nicholas. In 1841 Russia sold the settlement of Fort Ross in California to the US and it was also during the reign of Nicholas that the idea of selling all of the Russian colonies in North America arose in government circles.

In the exhibition we can see the Imperial court through the eyes of American envoys who described their impressions in their letters home. The English artist D. Dawe, who was invited to Russia to paint the portraits of the heroes of 1812 for the Winter Palace, portrayed Alexander I as we see him here. Elizabeth Alexeevna, wife of Alexander I was portrayed by a Russian artist and in this portrait we see one of the most beautiful, noble and poetic women of her time. She was a very modest Empress as well. A German artist painted the portrait of Alexandra Fedorovna, wife of Nicholas I, who was known for her love of beautiful clothes and balls. The emperors' personal things, palace furnishings and jeweled objects convey a picture of life in the palace. Each of these is a unique part of the ambiance of Russian everyday court life of the period. Furniture such as the steel chair that is exhibited here was designed expressly for the formal rooms of the palaces. The cold glitter of

steel furniture complemented the matte surface of ivory and walrus bone. The Russian aristocracy adored malachite which personified richness and was thought to heal depression and encourage reasonable thinking. It is quite possible that a young lady-in-waiting wearing a pair of the gold earrings adorned with miniature portraits of the beloved Alexander I and Elizabeth Alexeevna, excitedly met the glance of the most handsome couple in Russia. But she might have fainted at the glance of Nicholas I, a very tall man.

Before the Russian colonies in America were purchased by the United States, which occurred during the reign of Alexander II, successor of Nicholas I, our travelers will be introduced to the vast spaces of Siberia and eventually reach the shores of the New World. A traveler crossing the Urals which form the border between Europe and Asia, will enter Siberia. Here one can meet the Cossacks who discovered those lands and were among the first settlers of Siberia. Besides the Cossacks there were merchants and native populations who had lived there long before the arrival of Russians. The Cossacks are a very interesting section of the Russian population. In some ways they can be compared to American farmers. However, besides farming they did military service and guarded the borders of the Empire. They were dashing, courageous and sometimes even reckless people. They could never resist the desire to travel and explore new lands. Not by accident is the word "Cossack" translated in the Japanese language as "free and unrestrained adventurer." In the exhibition one can see a baton that is the decorative symbol of the Cossack chieftain's power. These explorers used travel utensils that testify to their nomadic life. And of course a Russian traveler would never be without his folding icon for protection in his travels.

Shawls such as the one decorated with lilacs in the exhibition, were made only in Russia. Serf girls with their tapered fingers and good eyesight spent the best years of their lives working on these masterpieces. Their mistresses were awarded gold medals at exhibitions.

The merchant portraits of a man and woman reflect the nature of Siberian traders and the characteristics of their class: stern, prudent, calculating and unhurried. They were hard working people, but they were also good at counting every penny and investing it at a profit. The government tried to encourage the Cossacks and merchants with awards such as medals and orders, for example the medal given by Catherine II "For work for the benefit of the country". She awarded these medals to 12 merchants who arranged fishing and hunting expeditions to the Aleutians and mapped the region. Siberian governors would also award precious objects to people who distinguished themselves. Governor Chicherin, who loved luxurious things, commissioned precious objects bearing his coat of arms, initials and portrait to be given to people.

Seeing some of the domestic decorations and furnishings of a Siberian merchant's house and also the dwelling of a peasant, the traveler will be able to discern the style of life there. Russians love to decorate their houses and domestic furnishings with patterned ornamentation. Carved window bands, architectural boards, painted chests, sleighs, utensils, embroidered dresses, etc, introduce the traveler to the world of Russian traditions. Amusing lions, mythical birds and horses – all these are the symbols and images of the language of the Slavic tribes that have survived to our day.

Particularly fortunate is the traveler who finds himself at a Russian wedding. Before the bride and groom go to the church for the wedding, where they are adorned with beautiful crowns, there will be a bridal party where he will meet the bride. One would be surprised at the unusual ceremony and the wildness of the women's costumes which Alexander I once came expressly to see. After the wedding ceremony one would be taken for a ride in a beautifully adorned troika whose bell can be heard even in the most distant villages. The bride and groom would ride in a small but heavy sleigh. There would be plenty of prianiki (molded gingerbreads) for the guests and strangers alike. Prianiki are favorite sweets in hospitable Russian households. Tsars and people of humble origin loved prianiki. They were made in different shapes and sizes and sometimes they were so large that a cart or sleigh was required to transport them. The prianiki in the exhibition are more than 100 years old, indicating how Russians cherished such things. The 17th century golden wedding chest held things that belonged to women in the same family for many generations. More than one generation

Fig. 6.
Painted wooden sled from the Russian North, 19th century.
State Historical Museum, Moscow

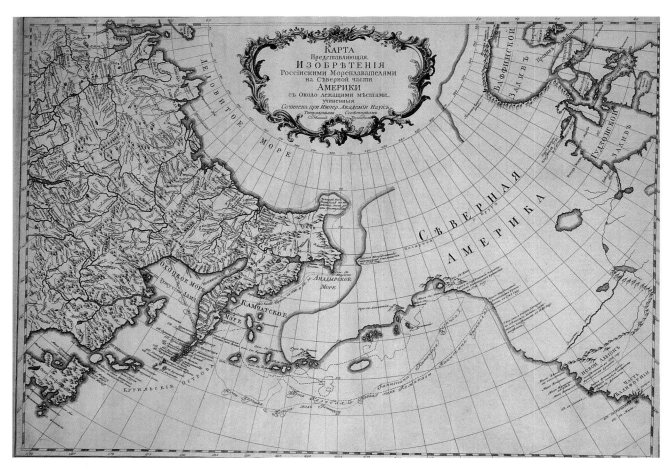

Fig. 7.
Russian sailor's map of North America
engraving by I. Truscott, 1754
State Historical Museum, Moscow

has used the old healing book that has found its way into the exhibition.

Russians arrived in Siberia when it had already been populated by dozens of different peoples such as the Evenky, Chukchi, Koryak, Yakut and others. Something of their original culture and beliefs is reflected in the formal costume made of leather and fur, the ritual ball that was a symbol of the sun and the leather mask that is the image of a water spirit. Russia's colonial policy was not always just and equitable, however it was preordained that these ethnic minorities were to become part of the unified Russian state and live side by side with Russians who imparted to them their centuries long experience and knowledge.

The difficult land route now becomes a sea voyage that is no less complicated for the traveler. The northern waters are very severe. American settlers are well aware of this fact, as they also had to cross the Atlantic before they came to the New World. Russian seafarers have always adorned their ships with symbols of good in the hope that this would help them in their travels. The representation of the sun on the mast, sea creatures on the cabin doors and sculptures of St. Nicholas and St. Paraskeva would make the voyage less dangerous and bring them good luck in their business. Maps and atlases compiled by Russian sailors and scholars in the 18th and 19th centuries are very impressive showing the huge territories and scientific information that they incorporate. A rare hand drawn ethnographic map of V. Bering's first Kamchatka expedition depicts 11 Siberian peoples and scenes from their life: hunting, houses, funeral rites, etc. The map follows the route of the tragic voyage of Bering who never saw the long awaited America. It is here in America that this 1780 map of the Russian discoveries in the Northern Pacific is being revealed for it has never before been exhibited. This same year – 1780 – was also the year that Catherine II refused to participate in the blockade of the United States. The map also indicates the expeditions and voyages of other explorers and Cossacks and the route of J. Cook's voyage in those latitudes. The expedition headed by Billings and Sarychev (1789-1792) was also of great scientific significance. They described Kamchatka and all of the Aleutian Islands, part of the American coast, measured sea depths and collected priceless ethnographic materials. By the Empress' decree this map was to be kept in secret custody in the Admiralty. Another map dated 1787 (only 2 maps like this are known) tells a story of Russian trade in the North Pacific. Here one can see convenient sea routes and the American coastline – bays, harbors, rivers, woods and settlements. The map inset symbolically portrays Russian trade partners, the god Hermes, Indians and the Chinese. For the first time the borders of the Russian colonies in America appear on this map.

Having crossed the ocean together with the Russian explorers, the traveler finds himself in Russian America. Here we meet three main characters who made the greatest contribution to the growth of Russian settlements.

In 1783 a trading fleet of three Russian ships owned by the merchant Gregory Shelikhov reached the coast of North America. They were the *Three Saints,* the *St. Simeon and St. Anna* and the *St. Michael*. Shortly thereafter, Shelikhov became the chief developer of these lands. But he was not involved only in business in Alaska. He also tried to convert the local populations and bring them into Russian citizenship, establish trade relations with Japan, China, the Philippines, India and Korea. In 1788 Shelikhov and his partner sent a petition to St. Petersburg requesting monopoly rights for their company. They tried to convince government officials that Russian colonies in North America and Russian expansion in the Pacific were of vital importance for Russia. Catherine II rejected their petition, saying that monopoly is "against my principles", "monopoly is a beast of a hundred heads" and "the American peoples and trade with them should be left to its own destiny". It was Gregory Potemkin who influenced the Empress in her decision. He had always held the Crimea in the south of Russia to be the focus of a strong official policy. Also, the Empress did not want a Russian variation of the colonial struggle for independence. "Trade is one thing," she stressed, "while ownership is quite different." However she issued a decree awarding silver swords and gold medals to Shelikhov and Golikhov in recognition of their services to the country. The only request that was granted by the Empress was to send Russian clergy to America "to preach the Gospel." Shortly thereafter, in 1794, a Russian religious mission headed by Archimandrite Iosaph was dispatched to North America. On October 5 the mission arrived in the harbor of Kodiak Island. This was the beginning of Orthodoxy in America.

Also important for North America was Alexander Baranov who came from the ancient Northern Russian town of Kargopol. He was a merchant with a great mind and strong will. He came to America at the invitation of Shelikhov to

Fig. 8.
Alexander A. Baranov by M.T. Tikhonov,
circa 1810
oil on canvas
State Historical Museum, Moscow

assume the position of manager of the activities of Shelikhov's company. From 1799 he governed the entire territory belonging to the Russian-American Company which had been approved after the death of Catherine II. Baranov constantly claimed new territories on the continent and founded new settlements. Among these was Fort Ross in California. Through American ships in the area Baranov traded with Boston, New York, the Sandwich Islands and Manila. As a result of his efforts several Russian ships were built in North America with the assistance of American shipbuilders. He also organized the opening of schools and orphanages and sent local young people to St. Petersburg to study navigation and shipbuilding. Baranov knew how to manage Siberian merchants and he advised those who worked for him to become acquainted with the local people "as soon as possible . . .in a peaceful and friendly demeanor . . .do not be rude to our workers". He lived in North America for 25 years and retired after 14 years of service. He died aboard the ship *Kutuzov* on his way back to Russia when they were near the island of Java. In accordance with maritime custom his body was buried at sea.

The life story of another hero who served as a link between the two continents is full of adventure and romance. The story of Nicholas Rezanov is closely connected with the Russian-American Company which was established on July 8/19, 1799. On that date Emperor Paul signed a decree concerning the establishment of the Russian-American Company under "the patronage of His Imperial Highness." Many believe that he made this decision to contradict his mother, Catherine II. Indeed after her death, he consistently acted contrary to her will. It is also possible that he signed this document due to the influence of Rezanov, who was Shelikhov's son-in-law, a Senate Secretary, passionate patriot and clever courtier. Rezanov was born into a

noble family in 1764. He performed his military service in a Guard's regiment and then worked in a civilian job. In 1794 he married Shelikhov's daughter, Anna. She died 7 years later and Rezanov was left a widower with two little girls. He mourned his beloved wife and it is possible that this situation prompted him to take part in the first Around the World Expedition (1803-1806) organized by the Russian-American Company. He turned to the Sovereign with the request to be appointed as envoy to Japan. Thus he became the head of the Expedition on the ships *Nadezhda* and *Neva*, whose captains were I.F. Kruzenstern and Y.F. Lisiansky. Both ships sailed under the flag of the Russian-American Company. Rezanov transported several thousand books for the colonies on the *Neva*. Arriving on Japanese shores they learned of the law of 1638 which stated that "as long as the sun lights the world, no one will dare to land on the shores of Japan, even if he is an ambassador." The *Nadezhda* was damaged during the voyage and the Japanese allowed her to enter Nagasaki Harbor, but only after the sailors had surrendered all of their weapons, gunpowder and cannons. Rezanov, however, was allowed to keep his sword. Six months after his arrival in Nagasaki, Rezanov met with the spokesman of the Japanese Emperor and was told of the Emperor's refusal to establish any kind of relations. Returning to Petropavlovsk, Rezanov received from St. Petersburg an assignment as an inspector of the Russian-American Company to the Aleutians and Northwest America.

Living in the Russian colonies he was impressed with the hardships of colonial life: there was a shortage of most commodities and the colonists lacked food and construction materials (e.g. There were 470 Russians living in Sitka). Rezanov decided to establish trade with California and to found a Russian settlement there. On board the ship *Juno* which he had purchased from the Americans, he headed for San Francisco. After a strenous voyage he landed in San Francisco, then just a small Spanish fort, in March, 1806. Rezanov engaged in very successful negotiations with the governor at that time, Joaquin de Arguello concerning the establishment of trade relations between Alaska and California. He was also able to buy food at a good price, which saved the residents of Russian America from starvation. San Francisco was also the scene of an extraordinary romantic drama which became the subject of a poem by the American writer, Bret Harte (see *Forgotten Dreams*, p. 13). It was also the subject of a poem by the Russian poet Andrei Voznesensky which became the basis of a remarkable musical *Juno and Avos*, seen in NY, that is still popular today. The 45 year old Rezanov charmed the 16 year old daughter of the fort commander. Conchita fell in love with Rezanov and his stories about Russia and when he proposed to her, she agreed at once. Rezanov obtained the consent of Conchita's parents but the Pope's consent was still needed for the marriage of a Roman Catholic and a Russian Orthodox. After a stay of 3 months in California, the time came to say good-bye. Rezanov left San Francisco on May 10, promising to return in 2 years, and hurried to go back to St. Petersburg. From Okhotsk he set out on a strenuous journey across Siberia. Tragically, en route he became exhausted, ill and died in Krasnoyarsk where he was buried in February 1807. Conchita waited for him, rejecting all other marriage proposals and after learning of his death approximately 2 years later, she eventually took the veil and spent the rest of her long life in a convent in Benicia, California where she is buried.

Rezanov's short period with the Russian-American Company had some significant results however. The administrative headquarters of the Company was moved from Irkutsk to St. Petersburg. Government connections with the Company became much closer when several members of the Imperial family became shareholders, among them Alexander I, his mother Maria Fedorovna, (widow of Paul I), his brothers Grand Dukes Michael Pavlovich and Konstantine Pavlovich, and others. Once again the attention of the government was focused on the activities of the Russian-American Company. The Company also contributed greatly to relations between Russia and America. Basically, all trade between the two counties was carried out through the RAC. Each year Russia exported to North America from 2 to 3 million dollars worth of goods, including linen, iron, copper utensils and textiles. In the 1840's one of the most important goods imported from Alaska was ice. The RAC owed its successful ice trade to another company: the American-Russian Trading Company headed by Beverly Sanders. This company obtained the exclusive right to engage in trade with the Russian-American Company. Nicholas I signed the contract. The two parties purchased and imported "ice, coal, lumber and fish." No other company or individual was allowed to develop, purchase or import anything under any pretext. The list of stockholders of the American company reads like a "Who's who" of San Francisco (L. Herman, A. Gay, S. Hensley and others). In St. Petersburg Beverly Sanders won the heart of Grand Duke Konstantin Nikolaevich, who played an important role in the sale of Alaska to the United States.

The Russian-American Company continued to play a role in Russian diplomacy. Although the first diplomatic mission of Rezanov to Japan ended in failure, the second diplomatic mission to that country led by Admiral E. Putyatin, who advocated expanded relations with the

Fig. 9.
Menu for the banquet in the Grand Kremlin Palace in honor of the Coronation of Alexander III and Maria Fedorovna
Moscow, May 15, 1883
V.M. Vasnetsov
Color lithograph

USA, was quite successful. Putyatin arrived in Japan accompanied by ships of the Russian-American Company.

Objects such as the magnificent gramota awarded to Putyatin by the Emperor which granted him the title of Count; the silver tankard commissioned to commemorate his voyages, and the desk set given by the Emperor to I.A. Goncharov, the well known writer who served as a secretary aboard the ship all indicate the high appreciation of the Russian government of the activities of the Russian-American Company.

We can see in the lives of the Russian Orthodox missionaries who experienced the severe conditions of Russian America wonderful examples of the victory of the human spirit. Metropolitan Innokenty was to the native peoples of North America what the brothers Cyril and Methodius were to the Slavic people. He is rightly called the "Apostle to America".

The Orthodox Church is the main custodian of the Russian heritage in North America. By 1917 the diocese had 461 churches, 309 priests and deacons and 600,000 parishioners. Herman, a monk of one of the first of the Orthodox missions to North America, was canonized by the Russian Orthodox Church on August 9, 1970, thus becoming the first Orthodox saint in the Western hemisphere.

Gradually, the influence of the Russian-American Company in North America diminished. Russia no longer derived any benefit from her colonies there and resistance from the local populations was growing. There were not enough Russians for such large territories: in 1860 the total number of Russians was 595, while the number of Creoles was 1,896. The number of Aleuts was 4,645. American influence was growing and the strengthening of relations between Russia and the USA had a continuing influence on the decision concerning the future of

the Russian-American Company.

The story of the Company is told in the exhibition through the portraits of its founders, directors and imperial stockholders. There are also samples of its goods, materials pertaining to the round-the-world voyages, unique clerical vestments made of reindeer fur which are being exhibited for the first time, rare documents concerning Metropolitan Innokenty, the drawings of Captain Sarychev of Alaskan natives. The magnificence of the vestments, the spirituality of the 16th century icons, delicate miniatures from religious books and other religious objects provide a glimpse of Orthodox tradition. Clothing adorned with fur, one of the main products of the Russian-American Company, can be seen in the portraits of two charming Russian girls of the 18th and 19th centuries.

From North America we go to Moscow for the coronation of Alexander II, who would liberate the Russian serfs and initiate many social reforms. The coronations of the emperors were always held in Moscow, the heart of Russia. The pageantry of the coronation of Alexander II, who was born in Moscow and baptized in the Chudov Monastery of the Kremlin, was unprecedented. All along the route of the Emperor houses were adorned with flowers, garlands and banners. All the bells of Moscow were ringing. Numerous carriages, beautifully adorned, followed the luxurious Imperial carriage. The London Times wrote that "The celebration was magnificent and amazing in every way. The affluence of a huge country was displayed with oriental luxury but in good taste… The glitter of pure gold, silver and precious stones… foreigners have hardly ever seen anything like it." Just a small part of that panorama can be seen in the exhibition in the painting of *The Triumphant Procession of Alexander II across Ivanovsky Square* and a portion of equestrian harness made for the coronation.

The favorable interest of the government of Alexander II towards the United States can be seen in Russia's position during the Civil War that helped to prevent attempts to intervene in the conflict on the part of other European powers. Russia was the only country that was concerned about preserving the Union. A squadron led by S.S. Lesovsky was sent by Russia to the United States and was received with great acclaim in the ports of Boston, New York and San Francisco. In the exhibition there is a written address of American citizens to Alexander II, expressing gratitude for the sympathy and support of the Russian government during the Civil War.

Moscow has always been known for its hospitality, particularly in receiving visitors. Several Americans visiting Moscow in the late 19th century have left vivid accounts of the hospitality that greeted them. Jeremy Curtain, Secretary of the U.S. Mission to Russia was a connoisseur of Russian literature and especially Pushkin. Speaking at a banquet organized by Moscow merchants, he proclaimed that "One of the most vivid recollections of my life will always be the fact that I was a welcomed guest in one of the most heroic and famous cities known in history." 1866 was a peak year in the development of friendly relations between the two countries. The United States Congress unanimously passed a resolution signed by the President that was sent to Russia through a special mission led by the Deputy Secretary of the Navy, G.V. Fox. He received a very warm welcome in Russia, especially in Moscow. Toasts were raised to President Lincoln at banquets held in Moscow palaces and private clubs. A.M. Gorchakov toasted Lincoln as "a man who sacrificed his life for the sake of duty." Alexander II raised a toast to "future economic and spiritual development between the two countries."Fox spent three months traveling in Russia. Metropolitan Filaret, head of the Russian Orthodox Church, received Fox at his residence at the Trinity-St. Sergius Monastery near Moscow, the most esteemed monastery in Russia. When Fox visited Prince Golitsyn's wealthy estate outside Moscow, he gave an American flag to the estate peasants.

Fox's mission definitely affected the decision on the question of Alaska. Grand Duke Konstantin Nikolaevich, the most liberal member of the Imperial family, was also actively involved on this issue. In his message to Foreign Minister Gorchakov, he explained that the accomplishments of the Russian-American Company were already a thing of the past and that Russia no longer benefited from her colonies. "Their loss would not be too painful." The Grand Duke suggested a friendly resolution of the question. In December 1866 a special meeting was held with the participation of Alexander II, who noted in his appointment book: "At one o'clock at (Prince) Gorchakov's meeting concerning the Russian-American Company, it was decided to sell it to the United States."

In 1867 Russian America was no more. However, the rapport between the two countries continued to grow.

The idea of close economic, cultural and scientific cooperation between Russia and the United States originated in Moscow. On May 24, 1913 the Russian-American Chamber of Commerce was established for the purpose of "closer economic rapprochement between Russia and the great American democracy." N. I. Guchkov, an entrepreneur and the Mayor of Moscow, was its head. The most powerful politicians, scholars, economists and entrepreneurs were among its members. The organization published its own "Bulletin of the Russian-American Chamber of Commerce". There was also a plan to establish a Russian-American Institute in Moscow. Speaking at a New York conference, members of the Chamber of Commerce noted that "world history has known no other country except the United States that in such a short time, has become a world economic leader. Americans are honest, decent and open in doing business. For Russia, with its colossal wealth, only American capital investment will do." As a result of the activities of the Chamber of Commerce, such products as

Fig. 10.
Gold brocade fabric sample of the Olovyanishnikov Association,
member of the Russian-American Chamber of Commerce
early 20th century
State Historical Museum, Moscow

Fig. 11.
Prince A.M. Gorchakov by N. Bogatsky
1876
oil on canvas
State Historical Museum, Moscow

cotton, sugar, tools and machinery, heavy equipment, arms and chemicals were exported to Russia. In 1916 the American-Russian Chamber of Commerce was opened in New York for the purpose of furthering economic and cultural cooperation.

The traveler who has managed to survive this strenuous and complicated journey will be able to relax in Moscow and enjoy the ambiance of a city that knows how to entertain its special guests. He will be able to see portraits of the Emperor, of Grand Duke Konstantin, of the Foreign Minister Gorchakov, of Guchkov, the most powerful entrepreneur – all of them saw the future of their country in a rapprochement with the United States.

There are very beautiful historical objects associated with various festive events: the court dress of the fragile Danish Princess Dagmar, wife of the future Alexander III, a favorite of the Russian people; there is also the gold encrusted uniform of the highest ranking official of the Court and personal belongings of the Romanov family, luxurious textiles manufactured by the Olovyanishnikov Company, a member of the Russian-American Chamber of Commerce. The relaxed traveler will be able to see objects made by the firm of Karl Faberge, one of the world's finest jewelers, and will enjoy viewing the original and elegant objects made in the Russian style, based on the traditions of old Russia. They seem to invite participation in a sumptuous Russian feast.

Each country has its own path. But all exist in one world. In order to understand each other better, it is necessary to know each other better. Perhaps the journey from Russia to the New World will be able to facilitate better mutual understanding between the peoples of these two great powers.

*Natalia A. Kargapolova is a Senior
Curator of Exhibits at the Russian
State Historical Museum, Moscow*

Forgotten Dreams
The Story of Rezanov and "Conchita"

James W. Symington

Of all the "roads not taken", none could have led to a more different future for the North American continent than the one charted by the imaginative and adventurous Russian nobleman, Count Nikolai Petrovitch Rezanov, and which came to an end with his untimely death in Siberia, in 1807. It had opened in Moscow when a few years earlier he persuaded, in succession, the Tsars Paul and Alexander I, that fortune and sovereign opportunity lay along America's northwest. Their realization would depend at the outset on the reach and vigor of the Russian American Company with monopoly powers chartered in 1799 by Tsar Paul and supported by subsequent Romanov rulers for over a half-century. In the winter of 1806 Rezanov, an officer and a major stockholder of the Company, having accompanied Kruzenstern on Russia's first circumnagivation of the world, left that historic voyage in Kamchatka to conduct an inspection tour of the Company's North American colony. Finding the sparse island settlements to be poorly administered and in bad repair, he instituted immediate reforms, including termination of the wasteful wholesale slaughter of fur seals (thus becoming the hemisphere's first conservationist), and a directive requiring clergymen to learn native speech. On the shelves of an unused building in the colony's headquarters on Kodiak Island he arranged the hundreds of books, maps, ship models, and scientific instruments he had brought on the assumption the colony was ready for higher learning. But it was not until he reached the Colony's principal fur trading post at Sitka that he saw the perilous state of the enterprise. Periodically beset by hostile Indians and debilitated by scurvy it was on the verge of extinction. Time being of the essence, Rezanov found and purchased an American ship, the Juno, with its entire cargo of trade goods (cloth, tools, muskets, finery) and set sail for New Spain's principal port in California, San Francisco. In those days the Spanish government had to keep a weather eye on a wide variety of potential competitors for the lush terrain of California, including British, French and the "Bostonians" the name given to describe Americans encountered on ships out of Boston. Highly suspicious of all such navigation along the coast of California, the Spanish government discouraged, if it did not forbid, would-be visitors to the port of San Francisco. Rezanov, himself, would have been turned away but for his pluck, guile, and determination to carry out his mission. After a month's sail with a scurvy-ridden crew, he reached the harbor of San Francisco, and proceeded as he later noted in his Report to the Russian Minister of Commerce, Nicholas Rumiantsev:

"Embracing at once the opportunity offered by a favorable wind (April 8, 1806) and the suspicious nature of the Spanish government being known to me, I thought it best to go straight through the gate and by the fort, in view of our desperate situation. I deemed it useless to send in and ask for permission to enter, since, in the event of refusal, we should necessarily perish at sea, and decided that two or three cannonballs would make less difference to us than refusal. With all sails full, we ran for the puerto. As we neared the fort a great commotion was observed among the soldiers, and when abreast of it one of them asked, "What ship is that?" "Russian", we replied. They shouted several times to anchor but we merely replied, "Si, señor, Si, señor", and simulated an active effort to comply..."

When the Juno was within cannon-shot of the Presidio, it dropped anchor, and Rezanov dispatched a young lieutenant with the message that they were on their way to Monterey on a courtesy visit pre-approved by the Spanish government but now delayed by storm damage. This fabrication produced a warm welcome from Lt. Don Louis Antonio Arguello, in charge of the fort in the temporary absence of his father, the Commandante Don Jose Dario Arguello. With the valuable aid of his German doctor and companion, George H. von Langsdorff, whose knowledge of Latin facilitated communication with two friendly Franciscan padres, Rezanov, Grand Chamberlain of the Russian Court, established his beachhead in California's "forbidden" harbor.

But the trip had already produced unforeseen possibilities and an expanded agenda, for as he made his way down the warm coast of California, noting its greenery and hospitality to plant life, it

Fig. 12.
Nicholas P. Rezanov by an unknown artist
early 19th century
oil on canvas
State Historical Museum, Moscow

occurred to him that Russian occupation of vast portions of that territory would be not only advantageous but relatively simple to accomplish. The British, French, and "Bostonians" were far from their bases of support, while the Spanish, with their sparse missions, had only a light hold on the vast interior, devoting their energy principally to the christianization of native tribes. Passing the entrance to the mouth of the Columbia River, Rezanov made two unsuccessful attempts to enter, and, but for unfavorable tides, might have raised the double eagle on American soil, unaware that Lewis and Clark had just decamped from Fort Clatsop, near the mouth of the river. He had heard of the latter expedition, but would not have expected its arrival so soon, if at all. Moreover, as he states in his subsequent Report to Minister Rumiantsev, "A settlement there would have been easier for us than for any other people". Believing that Spanish territorial concessions to America in the east and south would diminish pressure on California, he concluded that there were sufficient "reasons why I do not find it necessary to enter into any negotiations concerning this coast with the Government of the United States". He then puts the question, "Will you strengthen this territory? I shall be sorry if the Ministry will not look into it, for if we strengthen our positions the Bostonians will leave the country of their own volition." He goes on to say, "if you can obtain permission to trade with Nueva California, the company could, from the profits accruing, erect granaries and use our own system of agriculture and cattle-raising, and with our trade with Canton fully organized, we could settle Chinese laborers there." He probably underestimated the degree of purpose as well as the momentum of American westward expansion, but implementation of his vision would surely have complicated matters for the governments of New Spain (later Mexico), Great Britain, and not least of all, the United States. The first of these, being already in place, needed attention and mollification at once. So it was serendipitous to say the least during his six-week sojourn among the Spanish authorities, including the curious, often skeptical, but ever hospitable Commandante Don Jose Dario Arguello, and the colony's amiable Governor, Don Jose Arrillaga, that Rezanov, a 42-year-old widower, should encounter, court, and win the hand of New Spain's most desirable señorita, the Commandante's sixteen year-old daughter, Concepcion de Arguello, or "Concha" as she was known. Of her he writes in his Report:

> *Associating daily with and paying my addresses to the beautiful Spanish señorita, I could not fail to perceive her active, venturesome disposition and character;... dissatisfied with the land of her birth, she always referred to it jokingly as a beautiful country, warm climate, an abundance of grain and cattle - and nothing else. I described Russia to her as a colder country, but still abounding in everything and she was willing to live there... when I proffered my hand, she accepted."*

Although Concha's betrothal came as a shock to her parents they gave their consent on condition of the Pope's approval. For that matter, Rezanov had to inform the Tsar that he would marry outside the Orthodox faith. The pre-marital concord thus reached with the Arguello's, and their good friend, the Governor, provided Rezanov, who had brought his violin, the opportunity to display Russian hospitality. "The governor", his Report continued, "proving his sincerity, danced with us, notwithstanding his weak legs... The tuneful guitars of the Spaniards accompanied the vocalizations of the Russians... ".

Eventually bartering his cargo of hard goods for the needed grain, he had required but a month and a half to achieve his two original objectives, immediate provisions for Sitka, and an undertaking by the colonial authority to submit to the Spanish government a treaty for such provisioning on a regular basis. A third reward he mentions as follows in his Report:

"Should fate decree the completion of my romance - not begun in passion, which is not becoming of my age, but arising under the pressure of conditions - Remoteness, duties, responsibilities - perhaps also under the influence of remnants of feelings that in the past were a source of happiness in my life - I shall be in a position to serve my country again."

His departure from San Francisco May 21, 1806 was attended with ceremonial cannon fire and mutual expressions of hope for a speedy return. After replenishing the Sitka settlement he sailed on the *Juno* to Kamchatka, setting forth on his overland trek to St. Petersburg on September 14th. Stricken by fever along the way he pressed on through wintry Siberian wastes until falling from his horse. Unable to continue he died in

Krasnoyarsk, March 1, 1807. And with him went the likelihood, if not all hope, for the extension of Russian sovereignty on the American continent, a corollary being the sale of all Alaska to the U.S. sixty years later.

The projected treaty was never signed, and Rezanov, himself, would be forgotten in the sweep of history. What of his "Conchita?"

One summer afternoon a few years ago my wife and I stood by her gravestone in the Dominican Cemetery of the little town of Benecia. Once the capital of American California (1853-54), Benecia is now an historic site, nestled some 22 miles northeast of San Francisco. The cemetery is the final resting place of Dona Maria Concepcion, the once vivacious beauty who charmed a nobleman from another culture and clime, and whose influence might have altered the course of history and of nations. Her betrothed having failed to return, she entered the Dominican Sisterhood, and spent her last days as a beloved teacher in St. Catherine's Seminary, the first convent school in California. Her reaction, upon finally learning the circumstances of her lover's death is recorded as follows in a poem by Bret Harte which concludes with that revelation by the visiting British statesman, Sir George Simpson, at a San Francisco banquet in his honor.

The Honorable James W. Symington is a former Chief of Protocol of the United States and former Congressman from Missouri. He is currently a lawyer in private practice in Washington, DC

*Forty years on wall and bastion
swept the hollow idle breeze,
Since the Russian eagle fluttered from
the California seas.*

*Forty years on wall and bastion
wrought its slow but sure decay;
And St. George's cross was lifted in
the port of Monterey.*

*And the citadel was lighted, and the
hall was gaily drest,
All to honour Sir George Simpson,
famous traveller and guest.*

*Far and near the people gathered to
the costly banquet set,
And exchanged congratulations with
the English baronet;*

*Till the formal speeches ended, and
amidst the laugh and wine,
Some one spoke of Concha's lover --
heedless of the warning sign.*

*Quickly then cried Sir George Simpson:
"Speak no ill of him, I pray.
He is dead. He died, poor fellow,
forty years ago this day.*

*"Died while speeding home to Russia,
falling from a fractious horse,
Left a sweetheart, too, they tell me.
Married I suppose, of course!*

*"Lives she yet?" A death-like silence
fell on banquet, guests and hall,
And a trembling figure rising fixed
the awe-struck gaze of all.*

*Two black eyes in darkened orbits
gleamed beneath the nun's
white hood;
Black serge hid the wasted figure,
bowed and stricken where it
stood.*

*"Lives she yet?" Sir George repeated.
All were hushed as Concha drew
Closer yet her nun's attire. "Señor,
pardon, she died too!"*

Archaeology at Alaska's Castle Hill, the Colonial Capital of Russian America

Dave McMahan, Alaska Office of History and Archaeology

Introduction

With its commanding view of Sitka Sound, Castle Hill has long been a defining landmark of the local landscape. This rocky 60-foot-high promontory once was the colonial capital of Russian America and the location of events that shaped U.S. history. Here, during the summers of 1995, 1997, and 1998, archaeologists from the State of Alaska, assisted by students and volunteers, scientifically excavated early 19th-century deposits to recover artifacts and information. The Castle Hill Archaeological Project was designed to collect archaeological data from the soil prior to a major renovation to make the site more accessible to the public.

Despite extensive disturbance from past construction, the team discovered the buried ruins of four Russian-American Company buildings with associated floor and trash deposits. Archaeologists recovered an astounding 4,100 lbs. of artifacts (represented by about 300,000 pieces), which they are presently studying in Anchorage. After they've been analyzed, the artifacts will be stored at the University of Alaska Museum in Fairbanks. The information obtained from Castle Hill will create a clearer understanding of the industries of the Russian-American Company and the day-to-day lives of the workers (primarily Natives and Creoles).

Prior to the mid-20th century, Castle Hill was surrounded by water on three sides and was cut off from the mainland at high tide. It wasn't until the 1960s that fill was placed around the base of the rocky promontory, giving it its present appearance. Baranov Castle Hill State Historic Site, consisting of Castle Hill and a small surrounding tract, is now an Alaska State Park. Known to the Sitka Tlingit people as Noow Tlein, translated "Big Fort," Castle Hill is one of Alaska's most important historical sites because it is identified with events significant in national, state, and local history.

- At the time of first European contact (ca. 1795) clan houses of the Kiks.adi Tlingit Indian settlement of Noow Tlein occupied Castle Hill. Recent C-14 dates indicate that the settlement was occupied by 1,000 years ago.

- In 1804, following a battle with the Kiks.adi, the Russian-American Company founded the settlement of New Archangel (present-day Sitka) on and around Castle Hill.

- From 1808 to 1867, New Archangel served as the capital of Russian America. Castle Hill was the location of the administrative headquarters of the Russian-American Company and the Russian governor's residence during that period.

- In 1867, Castle Hill was the site of the formal ceremony transferring Alaska from Russia to the United States. A re-enactment and celebration of this event occurs annually on October 18.

- On October 18, 1959, one of the first official raisings of the 49-star U.S. flag took place at Castle Hill.

- In 1962, the site was recognized as a national treasure and designated a National Historic Landmark (NHL).

Establishing a Russian Presence at Sitka

In 1799, Aleksandr Baranov, chief manager of the Shelikhov and Russian-American Company in North America, constructed the small fort of St. Archangel Mikhail six miles north of Castle Hill, which already was occupied by the Kiks.adi. In 1802, as the relationship with the Russians deteriorated, several clans of the Sitka Tlingit attacked and burned the fort. Only a few escaped to tell the story to Baranov, who was away at the time of the attack. Determined to re-establish a Russian presence at Sitka, Baranov returned in September 1804 with several vessels and a large force of Aleuts. He occupied Castle Hill, which the Tlingit had abandoned in favor of a new fort about a mile to the east. This location, now in Sitka National Historical Park, was better protected from cannon bombardment as shallow waters prevented ships from approaching shore. Assisted by Captain Iurii Lisiansky on the sloop Neva, the Russians attacked the new Tlingit fort around the first of October. Following several days of fighting, the Tlingit abandoned the fort and walked overland, eventually settling in the Peril Straits area of Baranov Island. Unlike the 1802 attack, which involved several villages, the 1804 battle was limited to the Kiks.adi clan.

The Russian Settlement at Castle Hill

Following the 1804 battle, Baranov constructed a fortified settlement on Castle Hill, naming the new settlement Novo-Arkhangel'sk (New Archangel). By June 1805, the Russians had constructed eight log buildings with stone foundations, and 15 kitchen-gardens were being cultivated. Nikolai Petrovich Rezanov, a director of the Russian-American Company, arrived at the new settlement in August 1805 and wrote in a letter to the Russian-American Company Directors:

The fort is placed on a high rocky promontory, or kekur, extending out into the bay. On the left, halfway up the hill, stand enormous barracks with two sentry boxes or turrets for defense purposes. Almost the whole building is built of wood good enough for shipbuilding, on a foundation of logs and cobblestones, with cellars. The building is on a slope and the foundation reaches the water. Close to the barracks is a building containing two stores, a warehouse and two cellars. Next to it is a big shed (balagan) for storing food supplies, built on posts, and under it a workshop. Facing the fort and next to this shed is a good-sized warehouse (sarai) and a store connected with it built of logs and facing the sea. The wharf is between this warehouse and the fort. To the right, at the foot of the mountain, is a building containing a kitchen, a bath and several rooms for company employees. A big log blacksmith shop 9 sazhens long [1 sazhen = 2.13 m or 7 ft.] and 5 wide is built in three sections on the shore. In the middle section are three forges, in the other two sections -- workshops. Then comes the barn for the cattle. On the hillside above these buildings is another bathhouse. Beneath the fort there is one more bathhouse, with a room. On the hill is a temporary log house 5 sazhens long and 3 wide with two rooms and a porch. I have one of these rooms and the two ship apprentices the other. I have enumerated to you many buildings but the men were living in tents till the first part of October. As soon as a roof is placed on a building, they move right in. There are some broken-down Kolosh yurts in which live the native workers and Kadiak Americans [Rezanov 1805, in Pierce and Donnelly 1979:153-154].

Fig. 13.
Illustration of Castle Hill by von Kittlitz, from the Lütke voyage of 1826. 1997-98 archaeological excavations focused on the area occupied by buildings at the base of the hill.

Baranov and Lisiansky made a treaty with a Tlingit envoy in August 1805, but no published accounts describe the contents of the agreement. Tlingit history, verbally passed down through the generations, states that a peace treaty was negotiated through which Castle Hill was given to Baranov in exchange for a double-headed eagle badge. This is believed to be the same double-headed eagle badge that is now in the Alaska State Museum in Juneau.

Despite the peace settlement, tensions remained high between the Russians and the Tlingit. The threat of Tlingit attacks kept Russian cannons always loaded and sentries posted. The settlement had a continuing shortage of supplies and vessels, and an unprofitable trade in sea otter skins. The shortage of supplies would have been more critical if foreign ships had not begun to frequently arrive at New Archangel.

New Archangel: The Capital of Russian America

In August 1808 New Archangel became the seat of the chief manager and the center of Russian possessions in America. Baranov remained chief manager of the Russian-American Company until the end of 1816, when advanced age, failing health, and unfounded charges of mismanagement prompted a change in command. In 1817, Captain-Lieutenant L.A. Hagemeister replaced Baranov and appointed K.T. Khlebnikov as manager at Sitka. Lieutenant S.I. Ianovskii later took charge, serving as chief manager until the renewal of the Russian-American Company charter in 1821. At that time he was replaced by Captain M.I. Murav'ev. One of Murav'ev's first actions was to invite the Sitka Tlingit to return to Sitka, separated from the fort by a palisade. This calculated offer was made partially as an effort of good will, but also allowed the Russians to keep track of the Indians.

Between 1818 and 1830, virtually all of the buildings from Baranov's tenure were replaced with more substantial ones. In 1822, a new chief Manager's residence on top of Castle Hill was finished. Its roof was covered with iron from St. Petersburg, and the lower walls and adjacent floors were sheathed with flattened lead to deter rodents. Most buildings were covered with tree bark obtained from the Tlingits. An engraving by F. H. von Kittlitz, who accompanied Frederic Lütke on an 1826 voyage to New Archangel, depicts the manager's residence as a log building with a gabled roof. This 1827 illustration also shows two or more buildings at the base of the hill, where archeologists discovered buried ruins in 1997 and 1998.

By the 1830s, the manager's residence on top of the hill had deteriorated. Baron Ferdinand Petrovich von Wrangell, the new manager of the Russian-American Company, obtained permission from the main office at St. Petersburg to build a new residence. This new two-story residence was finished in April 1837. The next governor, I.A. Kupreianov, modified the construction plans to add a small observatory to the roof, along with a lighthouse said to have been visible from a distance of 20 miles. The new building, which measured 12 by 7 sazhens (84 by 49 ft., or 25.56 by 14.91 m), was the largest and last of the Russian buildings on Castle Hill. It often is referred to as "Baranov's Castle," even though its construction was initiated some 18 years after Baranov's departure from Sitka. The Castle occupied virtually all available space on top of the hill. It had furniture of sufficient quality to impress foreigners, and in many ways was the center of social life in Russian Sitka.

It was here on October 18, 1867, that Alaska was formally transferred from Russia to the United States. Following the transfer, General Jefferson Davis (head of the Department of Alaska, U.S. Army)

Fig. 14.
This Japanese Coin (Kan-ei Tsuho) from the Edo period (circa 1638-1868) may document an active but forbidden trade between Russian-America and Japan.

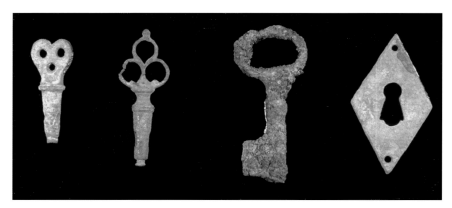

Fig. 15.
These keys, along with an escutcheon, were recovered in the Castle Hill workshop area. Metalworkers repaired instruments and locks in one of their two shops at New Archangel.

Archaeology at Castle Hill: Window to the Past

In 1995, archaeologists began a testing program to locate and evaluate buried deposits at the former Russian-American capitol. Initially, work focused on top of the hill, within a stone enclosure constructed in 1966-67 for the Alaska Centennial celebration. Most deposits were largely disturbed, but the discovery of a possible cellar floor from the Russian period suggested that other deposits of intact materials might be present. Archaeologists returned to Castle Hill during the summers of 1997 and 1998 to conduct larger-scale excavations in advance of construction work to improve access to the site.

In 1997, archaeologists removed and screened the soil from 52 one-meter squares on a natural terrace near the northeast base of the hill. The discoveries in this area far exceeded expectations. The archaeologists discovered undisturbed Russian period artifacts in a layer 10 to 18 inches below the surface, along with axe-cut timbers and stains from decayed support posts. Within this deposit, the excavators discovered the base of a brick metal workers' smithy (kiln) surrounded by copper slag and waste, a copper ingot, iron bar stock, and metal-working tools. They also found finished and unfinished sheet copper implements, along with scrap from their manufacture. The deposit yielded a large number of organic items – items not normally preserved in archaeological sites -- such as textiles, cordage, rope, hair, fur, feathers, leather items, worked wood, and exotic botanical materials. This remarkable preservation resulted from slightly raised soil acidity, a condition which slows the growth of artifact-attacking bacteria. Archaeologists believe that this unusual soil condition was caused by the large number of axe-cut spruce wood chips in the soil, fortuitously left over from the construction of log buildings.

used the Castle as his residence and office. The Castle burned to the ground on March 17, 1894, shortly after the building was renovated for U.S. government offices.

In 1898, on the site of the old "Castle," the U.S. Department of Agriculture constructed a headquarters building for the Office of Experiment Stations in Alaska. After the building was demolished in 1955, Castle Hill became a territorial and, later, state park. On October 18, 1959, the year that Alaska became a state, one of the official raisings of the new 49-star flag took place on Castle Hill. In 1962, Castle Hill was designated a National Historic Landmark. Since statehood, the site has been operated as an Alaska State Park. A ceremony to commemorate the transfer is held at the park on October 18 each year.

The organic layer contains a combination of domestic and industrial trash, mixed with materials from nearby building demolition and construction.

In 1998, archaeologists opened an additional 103 one-meter squares east of those excavated the previous year. Excavations in this area, beneath a heavily used park trail, revealed the ruins of at least four Russian period buildings. The floor deposits suggest that at least two of the buildings were workshops. One ruin, mostly destroyed by gardening and trail construction, is believed to represent the last Russian building to occupy the site. The metal workers' smithy identified in 1997 was fully excavated, along with the building that housed it. The intact forge was re-buried at the end of the season with hope that funding might be found for a viewing shelter and interpretive exhibit.

Archaeologists believe that, during the 1820s and 1830s, artisans and craftsmen worked in shops at this location. Manufacturing and repairing industries included coppersmithing, blacksmithing, shoe and leather goods manufacture and repair, and woodworking. The recovery of several modified bird feathers suggest that pen nibs were manufactured at the site as well. Concentrations of lead spatter in the soil document the pouring of musket balls, or possibly lead seals used in the bundling of fur bales. Under orders of the manager, workers labeled the lead seals with the initials of the Russian-American Company, along with letter codes to indicate the origin, type, and quality of furs.

Historic accounts indicate that Natives and Creoles (the children of Russian men and Native women) comprised a large percentage of the work force at New Archangel. Many Alaskan Native items were found in the workshop area. Ivory and bone carvings identical to examples from Northwestern Alaska were recovered, along with several stone dart points.

Items associated with the Bering Strait and Aleutian Islands Natives were found, along with spruceroot basketry and woven cedar bark matting of local manufacture. A notable discovery was a portion of a "Raven's Tail" robe. Only 12 examples of these rare goat wool robes are known to exist. Raven's Tail weaving was done by Tlingit Indians until replaced by Chilkat weaving around 1820. The Castle Hill specimen has design elements indistinguishable from those portrayed on Chief Katlian's robe in an 1818 watercolor by the Russian artist Tikhonov.

During the early 19th century, New Archangel became known as the "Paris of the Pacific." It was the largest and most cosmopolitan settlement in the North Pacific. The settlement was a port of call for traders who also visited Europe, Asia, and the Sandwich Islands (Hawaii), and settlements along the North American west coast. The Castle Hill artifacts include coconuts, hazelnuts, bamboo, and exotic woods. Three Japanese coins ("Kan-ei Tsuho") from Castle Hill may document an occasional but forbidden trade with the islands of Japan. Scholars from the Japanese Museum of Ethnology are assisting with the identification of these coins, which were minted during the Edo period (circa 1638-1868).

The Workers and Industries of New Archangel

Between 1799 and 1867, the Russian population in the American settlements ranged from 225 to 823, comprising less than 8% of the total censused population. K.T. Khlebnikov, chief of the Sitka office (1818-1838), recorded information on the population, buildings, industries, and living conditions in Russian America. His writings help us to interpret the archaeological materials from Castle Hill and, conversely, the archaeology adds depth and color to the written record.

Fig. 16.
This lead seal, inscribed with the initials of the Russian-American Company, was designed to secure the bindings on bales of fur. The opposite side of the seal is inscribed with the letters and symbols to indicate the type, quality, and source of the furs.

Fig. 17.
Lydia Black, Professor Emerita at the University of Alaska, shares insights with James Billington, Librarian of Congress, at Castle Hill during the 1998 excavations.

1 Office of History and Archaeology, Division of Parks and Outdoor Recreation, Alaska Department of Natural Resources.

2 The Castle Hill Archaeological Project was funded by the Federal Highways Administration.

The blacksmiths in Sitka worked at three forges, repairing sailing ships, making and repairing axes, and making plough shares for the California trade. The coppersmiths also had three shops, staffed by Creole apprentices and masters. They manufactured copper and tin cauldrons, cups, teapots, coffee pots, siphons, funnels, and other types of vessels in two of the shops -- for both local use and for trade in the outlying settlements. The copper forge uncovered by archaeologists in 1997-1998 was probably inside one of these two shops mentioned by Khlebnikov. In the third shop, coppersmiths casted small ships' fittings and bells.

Many of the specialized trades in Sitka were directly or indirectly related to the fitting and repair of ships. Coopers repaired barrels for the shipping of grains to the colonies. Less commonly, they manufactured new barrels, tanks, and other ship equipment. Woodworkers and boat-wrights made pulleys, blocks and capstans, pumps, rowboats, launches, whaleboats, and skiffs. Portions of barrels, pulleys, and implement handles uncovered by archaeologists may help us to better understand the scope and technology of these industries. A thick layer of wood chips at the site may partially relate to the construction of log buildings during the company's ambitious construction during the 1820s and 1830s.

Rope makers at Castle Hill manufactured various sizes of cordage and rope for logging and use on ships. We know from the archaeology that workers also used Native-made cordage of cedar bark and spruce root. According to Khlebnikov, candle makers made candles from California tallow to be used in houses and on ships. Archaeologists collected several tallow samples from candlestick holders at Castle Hill for analysis. Painters and assistants made paint from coconut or hemp oil. Both buildings and ships were frequently painted to prevent them from rotting in the damp climate. An active trade with the Sandwich Islands (Hawaii), and perhaps paint making, is evidenced by the archaeological recovery of coconuts in the Castle Hill deposits.

Public Education and Interpretation

Sitka had an estimated 200,000 visitors in 1997 and again in 1998. Some indicated to public officials that the dig was a highlight of their visit. From its inception, the Castle Hill Archaeological Project had public involvement and education as priorities. At Castle Hill, local residents were invited to work at the dig under the supervision of trained archaeologists. It was an opportunity to teach site stewardship and basic principles of archaeology. Experienced archaeologists and historians from other communities also participated in the excavations as volunteers. Castle Hill archaeologists collaborated with local groups to offer classes, lectures, site tours, and museum exhibits. The excavations have produced the largest collection of 19th century Russian-American materials from Alaska. The collection, due to its size and diversity, will be the focus of scholarly research for many years. The rich body of information contained within the Castle Hill collection may help promote a better understanding of the day-to-day lives and industries of the working class employees of the Russian-American Company. The archaeological data compliments the archival record, which focuses on important people and events or the broader view of history. The collection already is providing insights on architecture, trade, industry, food preference and preparation, adaptive re-use of material items, and consumer choices in Russian America.

Dave McMahan is an archaeologist with the State of Alaska, Office of History and Archaeology

Daily Life in Colonial Russian America

John C. Middleton

Introduction

The image most Americans have of the inhabitants of Russian America, if they have any image at all, is that of fur-clad, bearded men in tall boots, their wives dressed in the traditional long sarafan and kokoshnik head dress of pearls and metal braid. There are natives nearby in hats with wooden visors and gut parkas. It is a romantic view, created by writers who may be familiar with the history of Russian America, but not with the material culture of its population. The image has remained in the popular consciousness, and has even in some cases, influenced Russian research on the subject.

With the renewed interest in the restoration of surviving buildings at the historic sites of Alaska and California has come an interest in interpreting the lives of the inhabitants, and of restoring the context of furnishings, decorations, and articles of their everyday life. Archeological excavations and accompanying research as well as personal accounts and diaries of the colonists, now available in translation, are at last beginning to provide a clearer view of life in Russian America. Fortunately, there are more than a few surviving lists from the account books of the Russian-American Company. These provide much information on the type of food that was issued, the clothing worn and distributed, and the goods that were warehoused both to be sold to the colonists and to be used for trade. Comparing all of this information, along with company employment practices, infrastructure, hierarchy, and routines, with practices in Imperial Russia, one begins to notice similarities in both societies that have been previously unexplored.

Understanding colonial life is crucial to understanding the important part Russia played in the history of Alaska and California, and its context in American history.

The colonial period in Alaska of nearly 100 years saw many changes in the local life. Beginning with the private companies in the last quarter of the eighteenth century that became the Russian-America Company in 1799, and the later change from merchant to naval administration, the colonies witnessed dramatic changes during the period of tenure with Russia. It would be as unfair to single out any one period of that history as representative as it would be to have slavery define the American experience. The greed and cruelty of the individually formed private merchant companies of the eighteenth century are starkly contrasted with the enlightened administration that dominated the majority of the nineteenth century.

The material culture of the colonies in many ways mirrors this enlightenment, and is even mentioned in those terms by one of the colony's most noted explorers.

The image of the rough frontier existence has remained however, and has become fastened to our consciousness as have many other myths that we hold concerning our pioneer roots. They evoke a sense of heroic struggle that is consistent with the qualities that seem necessary to us in the founding of nations, and which imparts to those heroes an almost mystic relationship with the natural elements they struggled to overcome. The fur-clad frontiersman of American history heading out west has become merged with his fur-clad counterpart heading east from Siberia. It is a romantic image that will have to be abandoned to the reality of a raspberry-coloured, velvet frock-coated manager who reminded the company's employees of the instructions forbidding them to wear furs. The employees were artisans and clerks rather than fur hunters, who were concerned with the running of an international maritime trading company, headquartered in St.Petersburg, one of whose major stockholders was the Tsar.

Organization

In 1799, when Paul I granted the Russian-American Company its first charter, the chief administrator of the colonies was Aleksander Baranov. His position within the various ranks and estates which made up Russian society was rather low. He was a member of the merchant class with the rank of "Commercial Counsellor", roughly corresponding to the rank of a Petty Officer in the Russian Navy. It reflected the size of the operation he administered, and the number

Fig. 18.
Portrait of Gregory Shelikhov, founder of the Russian-American Company, wearing frock coat and wig in an etching by V. Ivanov circa 1795.
State Historical Museum, Moscow

Fig 19.
Portrait of Paul I, who granted the initial Imperial charter to the Russian-American Company, oil on canvas by P.P. Remezov after the original by Y.L. Voille.
State Historical Museum, Moscow

of men he commanded. Although the colonies had a considerable population, only a small portion was Russian. The chief administrator had under his command only those under company authority. This did not include neighboring tribes in the vicinity, or any natives that were not directly concerned with company operations. By the time the colonies were sold in 1867, the colonial population had increased to the extent that the Chief Administrator held the rank of Captain in the Navy. Although the territorial gains had not dramatically increased since Baranov's time, the population did increase, and the administrative duties required a person of considerable skill and experience who was recognized by the government.

Beginning with Peter I, Russia classified all her subjects in society on a "Tables of Ranks" which was created by Peter. The nobles held the highest positions with fourteen ranks from Chancellor (Field Marshall in the Army) to Collegiate Registrar (Sergeant Major), with equivalents both in civil and military life. The merchant class had three levels, with corresponding titles, and the townsman class had one.

The most populous class, the peasantry, was made up of serfs, who were either privately owned or belonged to the state, with no civil rights or position other than that. This system of classification was carried over from Russia to her colonies, along with the system of taxation. The only change came in 1821, when the company, with permission from the Tsar, created a special classification for "colonial citizens". This status was designed for the fast growing creole class (part Russian and part native) and for all natives who had become a part of the colonies under the colonial administration. It is an irony probably not lost on the Russian serf population in Russian America, that natives and Creoles could

hold the equivalent rank of townsmen in the Russian Empire, and enjoy a freeman status that was a rank above the Russian serfs who were not free.

As in Russia the majority of the colonial population was made up of the working classes. But unlike Russia, this majority was made up of state serfs who came from the north of Russia and Siberia, rather than peasant serfs. Their work was primarily concerned with fishing and hunting, wood-working, forestry, shipping, and unskilled labour. They were ideal for the purposes of a maritime trading company and their experience with the forests and rivers of northern Russian and Siberia gave them the needed experience for life in Russian America.

The first serfs and townsmen in Alaska were initially concerned with hunting sea-mammals for their furs and hides, primarily for the trade Russia conducted with China. As the colonies expanded, so did the need for self-sufficiency, and the need for a wider range of skills than hunting. The Company specified in 1820 the jobs available for applicants interested in employment: construction of ships and buildings; the felling of trees; the making of fishing gear; marine expeditions as well as trapping animals, and other duties; fishing and the preserving of fish, sailors, artillerymen, men to stand guard at the posts of the region, to work in the smithies and copper-foundries, or to do metal work—in other words to engage in all sorts of production. Almost all Russian serfs possessed many basic skills such as woodworking, building skills, animal husbandry, and gardening, taught from youth in their native villages. A specialized skill such as carpentry, blacksmithing, weaving, tailoring, masonry, or boat building would be added to his basic skills to prepare him for a specialized trade within his village or town.

Apprenticing to a local master crafts-man he would upon completion of his studies join an artel, or craftsmen's guild. Membership in an artel would connect him with others in his trade, and provide protection of his skills much as a trade union does for workers today. He would pay dues to the artel, which would establish accounts for the members, provide pensions for widows, orphans, and the disabled, and act as an advocate for the worker.

The Russian -American Company modeled itself on other state enterprises, which flourished in pre-industrialized Russia in the late 18th-early 19th century.

Employing an estate serf population, many landowners trained their workers in the winter in the production of various articles for sale throughout the country. Many of these estate factories produced a wide range of consumer and luxury goods such as china, shawls, glassware, cloth goods and furniture. Their organization helped form later industrialized centres in Russia, while retaining much of the character of the earlier estate factories. The serfs on these estates would be trained in whatever skills were required for production, and spend the non- harvest and sowing seasons in factory work. This way the labour force was constantly employed for the benefit of the estate.

The Russian-American Company followed this practice, and encouraged employment that allowed for various jobs as the season required. Thus hunters would also spend part of their time as carpenters; lumberjacks could be transferred to duty as farmers, and skilled workers such as shipbuilders would produce furnishings for houses they would construct. The colony's native population who learned Russian and became literate could become managers. This practice was found to be destructive to native village life, and so a policy was put into

practice with incentives to encourage natives to return to their villages after their employment with the Company. With the advent of Naval administration the condition of the native population dramatically improved. The first naval officers sent to the colonies in the first years of the nineteenth century were extremely critical of the merchant administration and its treatment of the native population. When the navy was placed in a position of authority in 1818, that treatment changed. Within a few years civil rights were granted to the natives, programs for the betterment of village life introduced, and wages and benefits provided in place of the contract labour system. A school curriculum was created which taught students in their native languages, and higher education opportunities were established for the Creoles who wished to advance their positions within the company

Daily Life

Descriptions by visitors to the colonies in the first half of the 19th century, and by some of the colonists themselves have given us a glimpse of life in Russian America. These scraps of information, collected from various sources, give the impression of a busy, multi-cultural population, which although small, was evidently industrious in attempting to establish a profitable concern in North America.

From the descriptions and lists one is tempted to conclude that the colonies were strongly influenced by the naval administration. Father Manuel Payeras, who visited Fortress Ross in California in 1822, described the regulation of the days with the tolling of a bell. His party was greeted at the gate by a sentry, welcomed with a cannon salute, and when they departed there were three cheers shouted out by the colonists. All these

Fig. 20A.
Flag of the Russian-American Company, Flown on all company ships and at colonial sites
St. Petersburg, 1992, reproduction made at the Vladimir Naval Flag Factory.
Collection of John Middleton

Fig. 20B.
People of North America with hunting and fishing gear, engraving by an unknown artist, mid-18th century
State Historical Museum, Moscow

practices, especially the use of a bell to mark the hour and half- hour correspond to the routine on board ship. Another visitor to Russian America, F. P. Lütke, made note of the watches, reports, reveille, and retreat. The lists of foods distributed to the colonists are also similar to the type of food issued to sailors. Among the "Rations for Promyshlenniks" of 1825 one finds such typical ship's fare as hardtack, and peas and barley for the making of porridge. Salted meat and fish also made up part of the ration.

Even the clothing of the colonists appears to be of a sailor's type, such as the linen canvas that was issued to workers and which corresponds to the type of cloth that was given to sailors. Their choice of official dark-green cloth for their festive clothing is consistent with what was issued to sailors. An illustration by Japanese castaways of the type of

clothing they were issued in Sitka in 1842 is clearly that of naval type.

While the labourers in the colonies wore clothing that was either standard issue or made from cloth issued on account against their wages by the Company, the foremen and managers presented themselves in more standard European manner. Many of the Creoles, who were educated by the Company at its expense, took jobs in management and dressed and lived accordingly. The men were described as wearing frock-coats, the women the latest European fashion.

In the capitol of Sitka and the various colonial towns of Russian America a pattern of life developed very similar to that found in small town life in Russia. The centre of the settlement was always the fortified compound of the administrators, where the upper and middle level managers lived and worked. Surrounding this compound was the sloboda, a village of houses usually found as in Russia, on either side of the settlement's main street. Most houses were privately constructed by the married employees, and had a courtyard and possibly a few outbuildings for livestock, a greenhouse and garden plot for vegetables. Unmarried employees usually lived in a dormitory or barracks inside the compound. Native settlements of company employees were always found outside the compound, and often formed a separate and distinct settlement of their own, with native forms of dwellings and customs. Natives not employed by the company often had villages neighboring the colony. As in Siberia, trade markets were held on certain days when natives could be let into the settlement under escort. These natives provided an important symbiotic function for the colonies, providing food and goods required by the colonists, and on occasion, a seasonal labour force for hunting and harvesting.

Fig. 21.
Koloshi, natives of New Archangel (Sitka) in Russian America, by von Kittlitz, engraving mid-19th century
State Historical Museum, Moscow

Except for a few attempts at creating inland farms and fishing operations most of the settlements were located along the coast of Alaska and northern California. Several of these settlements had boat and shipbuilding operations, and because of the maritime nature of colonial trade, they were active ports with warehouses, wharves and boat sheds. Near the water were the foundries and blacksmithing operations.

In Imperial Russia, a series of concentric circles radiating from the city's centre always defined one's social status and rank in relation to the distance of one's house from the palaces of the Kremlin. In Russia, by law only nobles could live within the city's centre. Merchants lived in town houses and apartments surrounding the centre, often physically delineated by parks and boulevards. Townsmen lived further out, in regions bordered by factories, and the serfs employed in factory work lived either in factory dormitories or in outlying villages. With the "Kremlin" being the fortified compound of the settlement, one can see the strong influence of Russian social traditions on the structure of colonial daily life.

As in Russia, in the colonies members of the lower classes could advance themselves through meritorious service to the Company. The first chief administrator, Aleksander Baranov, rose through the merchant ranks in Company service, and in 1817, before retirement, was ennobled and made a cavalier of the Order of St. Anna. Service in the Company, especially for the Creoles, was a sure path for social advancement in Imperial Russia. Some became members of the clergy, others captains of Company ships, still others officers in the Imperial Navy. For Russian Naval officers, the position of Chief Administrator of the colonies was always a good career decision. Most retired with senior rank, some as Minister of the Navy.

Even though Russian America was very far from the Imperial capitol, customs and appearances were kept up. The managers of the various settlements retained their ranks in the civil service, and had the uniforms and decorations of that rank sent out to the colonies. Administrators maintained their authority with the observance of the same type of discipline they expected in Russia. " The severity of military discipline is indispensable here in order to keep not only the Americans in check, but also the promyshlenniks themselves, among whom it would be well nigh impossible not to find some unruly and vicious natured men; these however, are carefully surveyed. The carrying out of orders, the receipt of reports, the guards, the patrols, reveille, and the retreat. All the duties are carried out in detail with a certain solemnity. Naval officers are always in uniform."

Various descriptions of the Russian colonies by both Russians and foreigners describe well made, attractive buildings, well tended fields and productive livestock, and gracious hosts. One comes away with a view of colonial life, which is perhaps more harsh and more restrictive than our own, but nonetheless is a more orderly and comfortable existence than we might expect on the frontier. While certainly difficult and sometimes even desperate in the early years, life in Russian America during the last quarter century of its existence, inspired bucolic reminiscences from Fortress Ross' last administrator, Aleksander Rotchev. "I spent the best years of my life there, and affectionately carry the memories of these days in my soul...."

John C. Middleton is an Historian of Russian America, Board Member of Fort Ross Historical Site, California, and a restorer of historical artifacts.

Fig. 22.
One ruble, 10 ruble, and 10 kopek marks of the special currency of the Russian-American Company, early 19th century, parchment State Historical Museum, Moscow

A shortage of a means of exchange in the American colonies arose from the very beginning. Even when Russian state currency reached the colonies it was not sufficient for the needs of the settlers. Consequently, on the suggestion of Baranov, it was decided to put into circulation new currency for use in the colonies. These so-called marks were used to pay the wages of the local merchants, artisans and natives. This currency was used in turn to purchase goods in the Company stores. In 1868, after the sale of Alaska to the U.S., the colonial marks were exchanged for Russian money. Some of these marks, however, have survived to the present day.

Mitre of a Bishop, Russia, early 19th century (detail)

The Mission of St. Innokenty (Veniaminov) on Unalaska

Marilyn Pfeifer Swezey

Well before 1799 when Paul I signed the Charter establishing the Russian-American Company, Gregory Shelikhov, who was already active in the territory of Russian America, made a formal request to Catherine II for a religious mission to Kodiak. On September 24, 1794 the first Orthodox missionaries – a small group of monks from Valaam Monastery on Lake Ladoga - arrived in Kodiak. The early years of that mission were filled with natural disasters of all kinds that gravely threatened the establishment of any missionary activity in Russian America. Only one of the monks, Herman, survived to spend 40 years in isolated existence on Spruce Island near Kodiak ministering to the small community around him. (He later became the first American saint of the Orthodox Church, canonized in 1970.) By 1821 there was a real possibility that the missionary activity begun more than 25 years before, might be lost forever.

Alexander I renewed the privileges of the Russian-American Company that same year and the new charter included a provision for "a sufficient number of clergy in the colonies". In 1823, Bishop Michael of Irkutsk, the city which had by then become the center of the Company's activity in Russian America, received instructions from the Holy Synod in St. Petersburg to provide a priest to the colony on Unalaska in America. The Bishop sent out a letter asking if any priest in his diocese would be willing to go to Unalaska. They all declined including Fr. John Veniaminov, a young parish priest in Irkutsk who, as he later described, suddenly changed his mind after hearing stories of the "zeal of the Aleuts in hearing the Word of God." "Suddenly," he later recorded, " I began to burn with desire to go to such a people."

After receiving the blessing of Bishop Michael, Fr. John hurried home to tell his family of this new ministry. "Kenia, Kenia! Guess where your feet are going to walk!", he announced, picking up his infant son Innokenty. The family tearfully begged him to reconsider, but in vain. In May 1823, Fr. John set off from Irkutsk with his wife Catherine, their infant son, his brother who would help to serve and sing in the church, and his widowed mother. They arrived in New Archangel in October of that year, remaining through the winter, and arriving on Unalaska the following July.

Here Fr. John began a remarkable ministry that was to continue for nearly 20 years. The Russian-American Company supplied him with a salary in colonial currency, an inventory of sacred vessels and vestments, liturgical books and all that was needed to convert the existing chapel on Unalaska into a functioning parish church. Fr. John himself built the iconostasis (icon screen separating the altar from the nave of an Orthodox church) for the church. But he also had to be a traveling missionary priest, and visit the many islands in the Aleutian chain. The Company supplied him with a two-seat kayak, a tent and native traveling clothes. With his faithful interpreter, John Pankov, a 46-year old chieftain of a nearby island, he traveled regularly to all the islands, baptizing, teaching and celebrating the Liturgy. In addition to visiting all parishioners and establishing a religious center, Fr. John set for himself the task of learning the Aleut language well enough to translate the Gospel and write a catechism for his flock.

The Veniaminov family lived at first in an earthen hut, then in a small house which Fr. John built with his own hands, including the furniture and the clock on the wall. During his long pastoral ministry his many talents revealed him to be a "Renaissance man", as he could be a carpenter, watchmaker, inventor, linguist and translator, naturalist and noted ethnographer, sociologist, missionary, teacher and scholar as well as pastor and shepherd of his flock.

At first glance, the Aleuts did not present a very admirable picture. But in time Fr. John began to understand them and perceived the patience that was their finest trait. He preached sermons to them adapted to their understanding, explained the meaning of the different Church feasts and the sacraments. But he never baptized them unless they asked him to do it. His extensive reports to Bishop Michael in Irkutsk provide a fascinating glimpse into the remarkable sincerity and dedication with which Fr. Veniaminov approached his mission. ". . .there was not a single village in which

Fig. 23.
Portrait of Metropolitan Innokenty,
engraving, late 19th century
State Historical Museum, Moscow

Fig. 24.
Petropavlovsk Harbor on Kamchatka,
unknown artist, 1803-1806
State Historical Museum, Moscow
Ships set off for Russian America from
this port at the far end of Siberia.
Kamchatka was part of the first diocese of
Bishop Innokenty in America.

I failed to serve and administer the sacraments, to teach the faith and law to each and everyone, and to explain to them the sacraments which I had administered. And they (the Aleuts) thanked – and still thank – me for this." "During the three years I have been here," he wrote to Bishop Michael in 1827, "I have considered my most important duty to be teaching the Word of God to the flock entrusted to me – and this I have fulfilled to the best of my ability. However, inasmuch as the Aleuts live scattered… over large distances, I have also made translation my duty. And so, with the help of God the Word, I have translated the Full Catechism into the Fox-Aleut language…."

It took a good part of the year to visit his entire parish, scattered over several thousand versts. He had to sail from one island to another and from village to village. There were privations and danger on these trips over the ocean waves in a little baidarka (an Aleut canoe made of skin) that was so narrow, that Fr. John had to hold his outstretched limbs in the same position for hours. He was very tall, 6' 3" in height. There was hunger and cold, sometimes being caught in heavy rain when he would be wet to the bone.

By 1834, just before his transfer to Sitka, he summarized his ten years on Unalaska and recorded his impression of his flock. ". . . no difficulty, no danger on the way – was able to stop me from visiting the inhabitants of this area. They are good sheep of Christ's flock – even exemplary, I must say frankly, in terms of their zeal, and rare in today's world for their zealous and constant hearing of my teachings. Furthermore, their simple, sincere gratitude for this is a tremendous satisfaction to me – and one of the greatest rewards on this earth." On his departure from Unalaska, Fr. Veniaminov recorded in his diary, "I delivered to all the local inhabitants who had gathered a speech which I had written for the occasion. It was on the text, *In a little while you will not see me anymore, and then*

a little while later you will see me (John16:16) – about how we will all without fail see one another there in blessed eternity. Immediately afterwards I boarded the ship, being seen off by each and everyone with sincere gratitude and regret – as witnessed by the tears in the eyes of every Aleut. That same day at one o'clock we raised anchor and sailed for Sitka. Thus ended my sojourn on Unalaska, lasting 10 years and 17 days (i.e., from July 29, 1824 to August 15, 1834)."

During these 10 years, Fr. Veniaminov had converted all of the inhabitants of the Island of Unalaska to Christianity. Although worsening arthritis threatened to bring his ministry to an end, he was to play an important role in Alaska for many more years. His mission among the Tlingits in Sitka proved to be much more challenging in spite of the fact that it did not require the extensive travel of his ministry on Unalaska which by the end, began to endanger his health. Initially, the Tlingits were not as receptive as the Aleuts, but in time his patient approach began to bear fruit as it had on Unalaska. He would often just sit and talk with people in simple, vivid terms. Soon he was in great demand and received everywhere with sincere hospitality. All those whom he baptized were held in high esteem by their fellow tribesmen. The number of converts began to increase among these intelligent and gifted people who had been mortal enemies of the Russians not long before.

All of this did not go unnoticed by the Russian authorities, even as far away as Moscow and St. Petersburg, as word of his remarkable ministry in America came to be known. Russian society learned about the work of Fr. Veniaminov through reports by Theodore Lütke, scientist and member of the Academy of Sciences, Baron Wrangell, General Manager of the Russian-American Company at one time, and sailors who had met him in the colonies. Also the steady stream of manuscripts which he had been sending to the Academy of Sciences (see *Notes on the Islands of the Unalaska District*, p. 35) served to acquaint people with the extraordinary Russian missionary in America. Fr. Veniaminov was greatly acclaimed by Metropolitan Philaret, head of the Russian Orthodox Church, who often said of him, "there is something apostolic about that man". The two became great friends. In 1839 while Fr. John was in St. Petersburg to publish his work in Aleut and Russian, his wife Catherine died in Irkutsk. After much consideration, he decided to follow the tradition in such cases and become a monk. He was tonsured by Metropolitan Philaret at the Trinity-St. Sergius Monastery and was given the name of Innokenty, after St. Innokenty, the first Bishop of Irkutsk.

On December I, 1840 the newly tonsured Archimandrite Innokenty was summoned to a meeting with Nicholas I. After a brief conversation about his work in Russian America, the natives and his life there, the tsar suddenly appointed him to be the bishop of the new Diocese of Kamchatka, which would include the territory of Russian America. While still in St. Petersburg, the newly appointed Bishop Innokenty was a frequent visitor to the court, where he would entertain the future Alexander II and the Imperial children with his tales of the people of Alaska, travel on baidarkas and other stories, quite exotic for them. Innokenty was consecrated bishop on December 15, 1840 in Kazan Cathedral in St. Petersburg and set off on January 30, 1841 for Siberia. The first stage of his trip was 2600 miles from Moscow to Irkutsk. He arrived in America as its first bishop on September 25, 1841. His first diocesan trip was a journey of 12,500 miles round trip from Sitka, which took more than a year to complete as the diocese extended from Sitka to Kamchatka and Okhotsk.

Bishop Innokenty has left a touching description of his reunion with his flock who knew nothing about the existence of bishops or that their former pastor had now become one.

"Several pages could be devoted to a description of how the Aleuts met me there and everywhere, and how I met them . . .But I will be brief. They met me as a father whom they obviously remembered quite well. (I will say no more.) And I met them as children, as brothers and true friends whom I love (now I am bragging) with pure Christian love. The first thing which brought me special joy and comfort was seeing with my own eyes that my translations into Aleut had not been stowed away somewhere but were being read – and even by the women, one of whom (a Creole) amazes everyone with her clear, intelligent and sensible reading."

He returned to Moscow in 1868 to succeed Metropolitan Philaret as Metropolitan of Moscow, and All Russia. In 1879 Metropolitan Innokenty died peacefully in Moscow. He was canonized by the Russian Orthodox Church in October 1977 as "enlightener and apostle to America" where his legacy lives on to this day.

Marilyn Pfeifer Swezey is an Historian of Russian Culture and Decorative Arts, writer, and educator.

Fig. 25.
Unalaska's Cathedral of the Holy Ascension constructed in 1896 near the site of the wooden church built in 1826 by Fr. John Veniaminov with the help of local Aleuts to whom he had taught carpentry.

Fig. 26.
Portrait of Metropolitan Philaret (Drozdov) of Moscow (1782-1867), unknown artist, mid-19th century, oil on canvas
State Historical Museum, Moscow

Documents on St. Innokenty from the State Historical Museum

Fig. 27.
Photograph of Metropolitan Innokenty with his son Gavriil and grandson taken at the Trinity-St. Sergius Monastery near Moscow in the 1860s.
State Historical Museum, Moscow

Excerpt of a letter of Hieromonk Feofil, Nushagak Missionary, to Archbishop Innokenty

January 20, 1859 (Cat.no.219)
Sent by Innokenty , Archbishop of Kamchatka, to Metropolitan Philaret of Moscow.
Russian State Historical Museum, Moscow

In his letter to Archbishop Innokenty Hieromonk Feofil describes the miraculous rescue of his keleynik (cell or room attendant), the monk Vasily. The young man and his friend, a Creole, went out hunting for geese early in October. Their canoe suddenly capsized on the river and Vasily's friend, who could not swim, soon drowned. Vasily reached a wet and swampy bank, where he was trapped. He was wearing only a thin shirt that was torn and it was already cold. Search parties were unsuccessful and hieromonk Feofil , who was very anxious and concerned about Vasily, began earnestly to pray for him. Vasily was found quite by accident by an Aleut five days later, very weak and near death from exposure. Vasily said that on the eve of his rescue he had a vision of the Virgin Mary as a young girl in a luminous robe. She said to him: "Do not despair, nothing is going to happen to you. You will be found because people are praying for you and anxious for you. Only in the future you must fulfill all the prayers and promises you have made to God." The next morning Vasily experienced extraordinary joy and comfort and by noon he was found. After he returned to his Nushagak cell he quickly regained his strength and within a month he was completely healthy.

This incident is described in I. Barsukov, *Innokenty, Metropolitan of Moscow and Kolomna in his collected works, letters and memoirs of his contemporaries* Moscow 1883.

A. A. Petrov

Message signed by Metropolitan Philaret of Moscow

Undated (Cat. no.216)
State Historical Museum

Judging by its contents it would have been written in late 1853 or early 1854. The document contains information on the marriage and ordination of Gavril Veniaminov, son of Innokenty. Metropolitan Philaret describes in all detail the bride selected by Gavriil Veniaminov, noting the determination with which the girl agrees to experience all the hardships of her future husband's missionary life. Based on the comments of the Archbishop of Kamchatka, the Metropolitan writes that the girl courageously endured all the hardships of the strenuous journey to America and also comments on her remarkable piety and readiness to assist her husband in everything.

This handwritten excerpt is quoted from *Innokenty, Metropolitan of Moscow and Kolomna in his collected works, letters and memoirs of his contemporaries,* by I. Barsukov, Moscow, 1883.

A. A. Petrov

Letter of Metropolitan Innokenty of Moscow to Bishop Leonid of Dmitrov

March 7, 1868 (Cat. no.218)
Russian State Historical Museum, Moscow

This letter written to Bishop Leonid of Dmitrov, vicar of the Moscow diocese is signed and dated March 7, 1868. It is the first letter written by Innokenty to his vicar. It was written at the Posolsk Monastery en route from Blagoveshcensk to Moscow. After receiving the news of his appointment as Metropolitan of Moscow he tells his vicar about the state of his health, complaining that his eyesight has become worse and he is no longer able to read. For this reason he is accompanied by his son Gavril Veniaminov, who serves as his reader. The newly appointed Metropolitan writes that "when I just think about where I am going, my blood runs cold and I involuntarily shudder." (The thought that he was to occupy the seat of his mentor, teacher, and friend, the great Philaret, as well as the thought of the service before him gives him a feeling of unworthiness and unpreparedness.)

From Notes on the Islands of the Unalaska District

Ivan Veniaminov

Editorial note: Fr. John (Ivan) Veniaminov arrived in Unalaska in 1824. In addition to his remarkable pastoral and educational work during the first 15 year phase of his missionary years in Alaska, he collected data on the geographical, geological and climactic conditions of the region of Unalaska. During the 10 years he lived in Unalaska he also compiled a detailed ethnological study of the peoples of this region. In 1834 at the request of Kyril Khlebnikov, a Director of the Russian-American Company, Veniaminov organized this data into several manuscripts to be sent to Theodore Lutke and the Academy of Sciences in St. Petersburg.

In 1841, he became the first bishop of Alaska and eventually head of the Russian Orthodox Church as Metropolitan Innokenty of Moscow. He was canonized by the Russian Orthodox Church on October 6, 1977 as St. Innokenty, Enlightener of the Aleuts and Apostle to America. (see Biographical Index, p. 93)

The following excerpts are re-printed here from The Great Land, Reflections on Alaska *with the gracious permission of the Limestone Press.*

Острова Уналашки Мужчина и Женщина въ народномъ платьѣ.

Clothing

The principal and most necessary garment of the Aleuts is the parka - a kind of long shirt falling below the knee - is now made of bird skins, primarily of tufted and crested puffins (sea parrots), but sometimes of murre, but, if these should be lacking, of (hair) seal straps, as Mr. Sarychev saw.

The parka for Aleuts in the local climate is an indispensable article. On the road it constitutes their bed and blanket and, one might say, home. With it they are not afraid either of wind or cold. This I can attest from my personal experience. Until I began to use a parka on my travels, I suffered very much from the cold and the winds, while using all means to keep warm which frieze cloth (frizy), even furs, and so forth, furnish. Their inadequacy is the

reason why, although one can see many Aleuts in frieze cloth or cloth (sukno) jackets and even frock coats (siurtuki) (as for the last, only toions and notables have them), all of them when traveling carry with them, without fail, a parka, and those who are more well to do even two, one new and one old.

Another and just as necessary Aleut garment is the kamleika, also a kind of long shirt, the difference being only that in place of a collar there is joined to it a separate hood or sack, which, in case of necessity in the rain for instance, is put over the head and drawn tight with a cord around the face. Cords are also attached to the sleeve ends to draw tight the sleeves. The Company makes kamleikas of sea lion throats (esophagi), but these are used by very few (people) because they are much too expensive.

Nothing can replace kamleikas either in terms of comfort or (serving) the purpose for which they were invented. This too, I tested by experience on several occasions. In the worst possible weather, a kamleika is light, warm and comfortable, and nothing could be better.

A kamleika, even the very best one, cannot serve as long as a parka. An active man needs two and even three kamleikas a year. (For durability the Kamleika is frequently oiled but never with fish fat.) A well-worked parka, of tufted-puffin skins, can serve for an entire year, as the saying goes, without taking it off one's shoulders (in constant wear), provided one takes care to protect it (the parka) from the rain. With care it can serve even two years, because it is not worn out so much as it breaks up from washing. Usually, for a parka, 40 tufted-puffin skins and 60 horned-puffin skins are needed. Marine animal sinew is generally used to sew parkas and kamleikas.

Formerly, Aleuts knew no hats or caps at all, and, in general, both sexes did not cover their heads or tie them up. Consequently when the Aleuts saw the first Russians, who covered their heads, they called them, before (knowing) any other name, saligungin, that is, the ones having caps or hats (shaposhnye or shliapniki).

Fig. 28.
Man and woman from the Island of Unalaska
in native dress, etching by an unknown artist,
early 19th century
State Historical Museum, Moscow

Fig. 29.
Woman from the Island of Unalaska
etching by N. Utkin, 1802
from the atlas of G. Sarychev
State Historical Museum, Moscow

Now, however, all men commonly wear visored caps (furazhki) made of cloth or (hair) seal skin, the visors sometimes fashioned of baleen and quite skillfully. Married women, widows and old women bind their heads with kerchiefs, and only young, unmarried girls go about with uncovered heads.

Shirts were wholly unknown to the Aleuts in former times, but now they have come into common use. However, not everybody has the means to own them. Prosperous Aleuts even wear waistcoats, trousers (of which previously they had no conception) and neckties. Wives and daughters of such men, on holidays, wear fashionable Russian dresses and shawls (which, because of their clumsy gait and stooped posture, sometimes appear rather comical).

The Aleuts use no belts except when it is necessary, in a parka or kamleika, to go on foot.

The parkas of small children almost always are made of eagle skins with (just) the down on them. For adolescents ordinary parkas and occasionally even frock coats (siurtuki) and dresses are made.

Aleut bedding consists of several tserely, or grass mats, one better than another; on top of these there are (hair) seal skins. In former times, in place of (hair) seal skins, sea-otter and fur-seal skins were used. Now many Aleuts have woolen blankets and down pillows, even featherbeds.

The Aleuts almost never wear gloves, except for old men, who wear leather (skin; kozhannyia) mitts on baidarka trips in cold weather. Instead of lining, soft grass is stuffed inside them.

To male attire belong the wooden hats or caps used only on baidarka travel. These hats are used specifically to protect the eyes from the seawater spray. They

are of two types, one with a closed, the other with an open crown.

The first are made from roots of three stumps cast up by the sea and are bent into the form of an irregular (elliptical) funnel. They are painted with different colors (in) longitudinal stripes and adorned with sea-lion whiskers, korol'ki (trade beads) and various carved bone figurines. Such hats in olden times, that is, when they did not have the present tools, were a great rarity. Only the toions and the notables could have them, as the best hat cost one to three slaves.

The other hats with open crowns are nothing other than large, long visors, like a crownless cap with a large visor, worn over the kamleika hood. Some of them are also adorned with sea-lion whiskers, trade beads and bone (ivory ornaments). The first (sea-lion whiskers) are usually attached on the left side only (in order) not to interfere with spear throwing, but those who are left-handed attach the whiskers on the right side. Such hats of large or small size are owned by every sea-going Aleut.

In a strong wind, large hats can cause the death (gibel') of an inexperienced person, since a wind can very easily get in under the cap and by its force overturn his baidarka. Consequently, as a precaution at such a time, many take them (the hats) off.

All travelers are unanimous in stating that the Aleut in full attire and in his baidarka has a handsome and indeed a majestic appearance. Then he is in his proper element. If the Californians are the best horsemen among Americans, then the Fox Island Aleuts are the best baidarka riders. No force of wind nor rough seas, and not in fact any impact by an outside force, if only the Aleut anticipates it, is able to capsize him, provided he has his paddle in his hands. The only thing which the Aleut fears--and which he is not able to fight--is a strong suloi (whirlpools and tidal rip) in the straits and also heavy surf at the landings. But in the latter case, too, an experienced and dexterous paddler can very often land or cast off and save himself as well as others. But in the first event, if he does not know how to avoid the suloi and passes between them, his doom is inescapable.

Food

Nature's bounty here is extremely meager and scant in terms of land products. The local climate hardly will allow introduction of any cereal plants. Consequently, the products of the animal kingdom alone constitute the food of the inhabitants here, predominantly the sea animals, specifically whales of all kinds (except the sperm whale) sea lions, fur seals, (hair) seals, sea otters, and to some extent walrus(es), and fish: cod, kalaga, red sculpin, halibut, Atka mackerel, sea perch, nalim, salmon trout, King salmon, Humpbacked salmon, dog salmon and silver salmon; mollusks: sea urchins, clams, black mussles, etc., and two kinds of crabs; birds: ptarmigan, geese and ducks of various kinds, murres, tufted puffins, fulmars, horned puffins, sea gulls, red-legged kittiwakes, and others.

In order to have a full list, let us include caribou, bears, porcupines (one Aliaksa and Unga), and domestic animals, that is swine and chickens. Of the vegetable kingdom they use for food: berries--crowberries (shiksha), raspberries (malina), and to some extent, other berries; roots: sarana, makarsha, chagitka, the sweet root, and sea cabbage (kelp) of two kinds.

At first glance, such an enormous inventory of the various products may create the impression that the inhabitants here have plentiful means for their sub-

sistence, approaching even luxury. In reality, their food supply is very limited and even scant, because, in general, it depends upon circumstances and chances incomparably more unpredictable than for inhabitants of terra firma. And there is nothing which could always be, so to speak, fundamental and unfailing food--with the exception of the water and air. It is even impossible to define exactly what is the Aleuts' staple food (what they eat most). In the best of summers, no more than 500 of the seasonal fish are stored for each family, and although ocean fish in many localities are abundant, means and circumstances do not permit the Aleuts to store much because the only possible method of fish preservation is by (air) drying, to which the weather, however, very often is an impediment. In winter the fish go into the deep waters, (and) strong and almost incessant winds do not permit going out after them.

Very few sea lions are taken, and in few localities. (Hair) seals, although they are found everywhere, are but few in number. Fur seals are only on the Pribylov Islands, while the sea otters are here only in the summer and besides are consumed by the hunters themselves.

The whales in summer sometimes are in great numbers, but only at Unalashka and to some extent at Akun. There, although they hunt or wound from 30 to 60 every year, no more than 33 and sometimes no more than 120 come to hand. Certainly, to the eye, 10 or 20 whales comprise a hugh quantity, but generally the whales here are only of the small kind so that it is easily possible to load a whole whale into one baidarka. Besides, even with the greatest abundance of whales, only inhabitants of the immediate vicinity obtain stores of whale meat and blubber, and then such stores are not rich. Their reserve never lasts a whole year, because some are careless and waste it to no purpose, others live too

Fig. 30.
Man from the Island of Unalaska, etching by N. Utkin, 1802, from the atlas of G. Sarychev State Historical Museum, Moscow

open handedly beginning with the autumn, but more so because there are no containers in which the blubber could be preserved. Since 1828 there have been rats here, which sometimes in one night strip the householder of his whole year's reserve.

Wooden vessels are very few because, although many of the Aleuts could make them for themselves, there are no necessary materials available (specifically hoops).

The main food of the Aleuts is fat (zhir-oil, blubber) of any (sea) animal except the sperm whale.

However many fish an Aleut puts up, if, at the same time he has no fat, one can say with certainty that he is going to suffer either from actual hunger or illness, because with long usage yukola, or dried fish, without fat is not too nourishing. On the other hand, even if an Aleut does not have a single dried fish, if fat is sufficient,

he will not experience hunger. Because with fat, he can use everything--roots, sea cabbage. Those who believe that the plentiful and abundant Aleut food consists predominantly of fish are in error. True, they eat more fish than meat, but this is due, however, only to the scarcity of marine animals. Besides, whenever possible they always eat fish only with fat.

The best Aleut dishes are crowberries with fat, beaten until white; the heads and fatty parts of the halibut. The second mentioned dish especially is considered excellent eating which even one accustomed to Russian cooking will not refuse.

The Aleuts eat almost everything raw except codfish, which, raw--and particularly not completely cooked is very harmful. The meat of sea mammals, though cooked, or rather stone boiled, may be said only to be warmed up.

They use absolutely no salt on food. Only nowadays, those who are workers in the main village have begun to use salted fish, but this is only from necessity. But no one refuses bread, tea and sugar.

Although the Aleuts eat almost everything and are not too fastidious about cleanliness, still, for all that, it is not possible to call them omnivorous--as they say about the Kamchadals--because there are things produced by their land which they absolutely do not eat, for example, mushrooms of any kind in any form. Also, at first when they saw that for several vegetables the Russians manured the land with ordinary dung, they did not want to eat vegetables which were produced in such soil. Even nowadays, when they have become accustomed to seeing this, they themselves will not do it even if there is a need.

To lay in fish for yukola is always woman's work. For this purpose they settle with their children in good time along certain rivers in which fish are especially plentiful. Each party is

Fig. 31.
Unalaska is one of the largest islands of the Aleutians and was described by Veniaminov as a "kingdom of eternal autumn". Unalaska's Bunker Hill looks out on Dutch Harbor, which today is one of the busiest fishing ports in America.

accompanied by one or two of the elderly or ailing men, not so much to help with the fishing itself as with the transportation of the indispensable things and to guard them from the vagabonds (beglye).

Laying up food for the Aleuts, it can be said, does not constitute the sole object or the exclusive aim of their existence, as it is possible to say about very many Russians of the common people if one looks upon both from such a point of view. Every Aleut lays up food for himself, but he stocks it up as if he worked for hire and not for himself, and as was said earlier, having put by a supply for two or three months, he meets the winter without a care. Notwithstanding the fact that each spring teaches him in the most intelligible manner to be more active and careful about storing food, he does not learn from such lessons. This lack of concern springs from the fact that living by the sea, this inexhaustible and rich storehouse for all around it, available always, they expect at every season to obtain something from it if only the circumstances and the available means would permit. Consequently, such unconcern of the Aleuts about storing food for themselves is, on the one hand, laudable, because, more or less, it is a sign of trust in All-Sustaining God. On the other hand, however, this attitude is by no means superior to that type of care which has as its sole concern only the stomach: it can serve as an excuse for idleness, and idleness is always worse than any bustling about and carefulness.

With the exception of supper, the Aleuts have almost no regular times for eating. They never eat in the morning, especially before a long voyage, in order, they say, to drink less, as otherwise they will suffer a serious shortness of breath.

During a voyage they eat very rarely and very little and just, so to say, snack on this or that. At the camp, however, they set free their appetitive, but it is not true, as some say, that they eat all night without interruption and that one eats as much as ten. True, one ordinary portion must take into account their uninterrupted labor and fasting, which lasts sometimes up to 18 consecutive hours. At ordinary times, in general, Aleuts eat very moderately, even less, it appears, than (they) ought.

All the mollusks, and especially sea urchins, which are used for food in great quantity, cause excessive drowsiness.

The only drink of the Aleuts is water. Until the Russians came, they knew nothing intoxicating, but since then they have come to know vodka and tobacco, which, in some way, replaces intoxicants (khmel'noe).

Vodka and all spirit beverages the Aleuts call tangam dagulga, that is, fool's for stupefying water. Now the use of tea, even daily, is spreading. They get it from the Russians in exchange for work or fish and so forth. The habit of drinking tea is growing so strong among Aleuts that many are ready to exchange a shot of vodka for a cup of tea.

Tobacco is in general use nowadays and for the most part as lemeshina (chewing tobacco), that is, it is put behind the lip. A few take snuff, but no one smokes.

Translated by Lydia T. Black and R. H. Geohegan

Opposite page: Gramota with Seal awarded by Alexander II to General Adjutant, Vice-Admiral E.V. Putiatin granting the Title of Count. Given for the signing of an agreement with Japan, St. Petersburg, 1869

Color Illustrations and Annotations

Fig. 32
Silver Sculpture – Peter I and his Botik
Model by Mark Antokolsky, base, Paris, firm of Falise
1891-1896
Silver
69 x 85 x 45 cm
State Historical Museum 68257/8925

Commissioned by Grand Duke Vladimir Alexandrovich to commemorate the 200th anniversary of the Russian Navy, the standing silver sculpture of Peter the Great on his botik is a monumental example of the decorative art of the early 20th century. Peter is shown on a stylized version of the old English boat that he found in a warehouse on the grounds of the Romanov estate at Izmailovo near Moscow in 1688 and which he later called the "Grandfather of the Russian Navy". Peter is seen holding a steering wheel and the boat is mounted on a stylized wave that serves as a base for the sculpture.

As President of the Imperial Academy of Arts, Grand Duke Vladimir gave the commission to Mark Matveevich Antokolsky (Mordukh Matisovich) (1843-1902), a professor and outstanding master of the Russian school of sculpture in the late 19th –early 20th century. Antokolsky worked primarily in small size bronze sculptures with inlay and enamel and also in silver. He specialized in Russian historical figures and famous personalities. Yaroslav the Wise, Dmitry Donskoi, Ivan III and Peter the Great are just a few of the historical figures that he sculpted. In 1878 Antokolsky was awarded the Medal of Honor and Legion of Honor in Paris for his works "The Last Breath" and "The Head of St. John the Baptist".

About Peter the Great, Antokolsky wrote in his autobiography: "He (Peter) was not just one person but a molding of several characters. Everything about him was extraordinary: he was unusually tall, unusually strong and unusually intelligent. . . his family was Russia." In the opinion of V. Stasov, "Peter I by Antokolsky is the best known image of this great man" who is perceived as a symbol of Russia opening a new European page of its history.

The base of waves was made in Paris by the famous jeweler Lucien Falise. The firm was founded by Alexis Falise (1811 - 1898) and was later expanded by his son Lucien (1838 - 1897). They made an important contribution to jewelry in the second half of the 19th century, especially in the production of enameled jewelry.

Russia and France had very cordial relations from the second half of the 19th century until the beginning of the 20th century. Emperor Alexander III adored France and even gave a bridge to Paris. The emperor considered the bridge a symbol of close political and cultural relations between the two countries. During this period cultural contacts were intensified: international exhibitions, "Russian seasons" in Paris, and cultural exchange between the two countries. This superb commemorative piece created by a renowned Russian sculptor and a French firm famous for its silverwork, is a powerful representation of the sea power of the Russian Empire at that time and also of the union of Russia and France.

G. Smorodinova

Fig. 33.
Masquerade Sleigh
Russia, late 18th century
Wood, iron, leather, velvet, galloon trim,
carving, gilding
312 x 120 x 186
State Historical Museum 58296/1492

Fig. 34.
Catherine II in Russian Costume
Late 18th century
Unknown artist, from the original by
S. Torelli
Oil on canvas
68 x 51.2 cm
State Historical Museum 16844/3296

The form and décor of the sleigh resemble an ancient triumphal chariot. The body of the sleigh is in the shape of a seashell which is placed on the runners. On top of the runners, which are joined, is a carved sculpture of a dolphin devouring a snake. The sleigh is decorated with sculptured images of the Roman Goddess Minerva and cupids playing with a lion. Minerva is shown leaning on a spear, wearing a helmet and an armored vest with two cupids, symbols of a wise and just female warrior who is a patron of the arts and crafts, well loved both on earth and in heaven. The image of Minerva was very popular in the age of Catherine the Great and was commonly identified with the empress. The sleigh is thought to have been made for a glorious masked pageant "Triumphant Minerva" that was produced in 1763 for the coronation ceremony of Catherine the Great.

Y. Fagurel

Since the 16th century the city of Tula, located about 120 miles south of Moscow, has been renowned as a center of metalwork. In 1712, in compliance with a decree of Peter I, an armaments factory was established in Tula which was to become a major Russian center for the manufacturing of arms and weapons. In their leisure time the Tula armorers manufactured a great variety of goods, including formal weapons, furniture, candlesticks, inkwells, chests and boxes, and snuffboxes.

In the decoration of steel, the Tula craftsmen used a technique for burnishing steel in a special forge which enabled them to achieve various shades and tints, from dark green and blue to purple, blue and pink. When the polished steel surface was tinted and gilded bronze was applied, the subtle effects of color could be achieved. The enchanting glitter of polished steel and the splendor of steel "diamonds" created by the Tula masters never failed to attract the attention of the Imperial court and Russian nobility. Beginning in the 1740's the armorers were continually commissioned to manufacture furniture for the palace interiors.

The artistry of the Tula armorers reached a peak in the second half of the 19th century as they mastered numerous techniques of adorning steel enabling them to create genuine masterpieces. Tula steel of that period is often compared with the work of English craftsmen, who used similar techniques of working with steel.

Catherine II regularly visited Tula and took the armory under her special patronage. Each time the empress came to the city she was showered with gifts, usually things made of glittering steel. At the annual fair held near her residence in Tsarskoye Selo, the empress purchased many things made of steel. Among the gifts presented to foreign ambassadors she always included some Tula steel items.

Unfortunately, the unique art of Tula steel work was gradually lost in the late 19th and early 20th century. But it remains a unique and original branch of the decorative and applied arts.

There are Tula art objects in the collections of many Russian museums. The Hermitage has the richest collection of Tula artifacts (about 300 examples), while the State Historical Museum collection includes about 200 examples. There are also Tula works in museums of Germany, England, France and the United States.

L. Dementyeva

Fig. 35.
Tula Seal
Early 19th century
Steel, polishing and burnishing
7.5 x 5.5 cm
State Historical Museum 5437/2011

Fig. 36.
Portrait of Empress Alexandra Fedorovna
Circa 1830
Franz Krueger (1798-1860)
Oil on canvas
135 x 92 cm
State Historical Museum 91989/3965

Alexandra Fedorovna (Fredericka-Louisa-Charlotte-Wilhemina) was the daughter of the Prussian King Frederick-William III. In 1817 she married Grand Duke Nicholas Pavlovich and in 1825 became empress. From 1828 she was the patroness of the charitable and educational activity of the Dowager Empress Maria Fedorovna, (widow of Paul I (1759-1828).

Contemporaries noted the beauty of Alexandra Fedorovna and her love of elegant things. As A.F. Tyutcheva, lady-in-waiting of Maria Alexandrovna, bride of the Tsarevich, noted, "For the Empress, the world surrounding her all-powerful spouse was fantastic, a world of magnificent palaces, elegant gardens, charming villas; a world of enchanting balls and spectacles filled the entire horizon...."

Shown in the portrait is the style of Russian court dress that became a tradition at court by the Ukaz (law) of the Emperor in 1834. It was required dress for festive occasions: "On important holidays and special celebrations... men were in parade uniform and women in court dress, that is the prescribed sarafan with a train, with gold stitching which made a magnificent impression. Such a ceremonial came to be known as the great entrance.' (A.F. Tyutcheva)

The portrait of the Empress in Russian court dress by F. Krueger was very popular and was frequently copied.

N. Perevezentseva

Fig. 37.
Vestment of an Orthodox Deacon (Stichar)
Russia, early 19th century
Silver brocade, velvet, silk, gold thread
142 cm long
State Historical Museum 80283/140

The vestment is made of silver brocade with a woven pattern in gold thread, velvet cord and colored silk of floral bouquets in vases, floral garlands, foliage, beads, peacock and ostrich feathers. The fabric was manufactured by a Russian silk factory in a Moscow province. The stichar is decorated with Russian-made gold and silver galloon trim and silk braid. A cross is embroidered in gold and silver with foil and sequins. The vestment has nine metal buttons and a cotton lining.

The reforms of Peter I in the early 18th century intensified the fast developing silk industry in Russia. Merchants from the Orient (China, Persia), and from Western Europe (France, Italy) brought their silk to Moscow where artisans had been making gold and silver thread since ancient times. Several silk factories in Moscow manufactured brocade in the 18th century and the Moscow province became a center of the Russian silk industry. In those days brocade was in great demand. It was used for church vestments and vessels and the church was a prominent consumer of gold fabrics.

Small artisan shops merged into large textile factories at the end of the 18th and early 19th centuries. Those factories manufactured gold and silver thread as well as decorative trims such as pearls and spangles. The firm of Vladimir Alexeyev founded in 1785 gained the greatest popularity in the textile industry.

O. G. Gordeyeva

Fig. 38.
Prayer Gospel
Moscow, 1810
Silver, velvet, enamel, glass, paper
23.5 x 18 x 5 cm
State Historical Museum 42567/8607

Fig. 39.
Icon of St. Nicholas with Oklad
Early 18th century
Wood, tempera, gold, silver, emeralds, glass, velvet
20.7 x 17.4 cm
State Historical Museum 1716/8138

Fig. 40.
Icon of the "Shuisky Virgin of Smolensk"
in a beaded oklad
Russia
second half of the 18th century
Wood, tempera, canvas, oklad of glass
beads and embroidery
30 x 25 cm
State Historical Museum 55753-9
BIS 1208-1,2

The Shuisky Virgin of Smolensk is a version of the famous Smolensk Odigitria, which according to legend was one of the three icons painted by the Holy Evangelist Luke and blessed by the Virgin herself. The Smolensk Odigitria has been, since 1811, in ancient Smolensk, a city that had been for many centuries a Russian outpost protecting the country from invaders. Odigitria, that is one who leads the way, has been honored as a Defender against illnesses, and a special help during times of national disasters. The Smolensk Odigitria is renowned for many miracles. Even some of the numerous copies have been known to be wonderworking.

In 1654 – 1655, there was an epidemic of a fatal disease in the central Russian city of Shuya, which killed thousands of people. In an attempt to be saved, some pious citizens decided to commission the best iconographer to do an icon of the Virgin of Smolensk. He worked diligently for a week, while all the believers fasted and devoutly prayed. When the icon was installed in the church the plague ended. As time passed, miracles of healing in connection with this icon became more numerous. And there were many copies made of the Shuisky Odigitria.

The Shuisky icon differs from the Smolensk icon in that the child's leg is bent higher and is more visible. The feast day of the Shuisky icon of Smolensk is July 28, as it is with all of the icons of the Smolensk Odigitria. It is also celebrated in commemoration of the end of a cholera epidemic in 1831. November 2, the date of the completion of the icon, is also commemorated as well as Easter Tuesday, the day of the first healing miracle. Another commemorative day is the first Sunday of the Peter and Paul fast. The many holidays honoring the icon corresponds to the long list of its many images both in churches (the Shuisky Odigitria was in the Moscow Church of Sts. Peter and Paul beyond the Yauza) and in private residences.

The oklad or icon frame is made of canvas embroidered with glass and beads, visually enhancing the brilliance of the image. The festive combination of rich maroon, blue, and green beading with the clear brilliance of the colorless glass beads touchingly contrasts with the defenseless, little visible leg of the Child. Such an oklad could have been made by a lady of the house herself as according to tradition, even the most intellectual women should not spend too much time in leisure. Devout women donated their needlework to churches or gave it as gifts to their loved ones, or even presented it to the sovereigns or church hierarchs. The oklad of the icon might have been been produced in this way as it is made of expensive beads that were particularly fashionable in the second half of the 18th century.

The glass beads used by this unknown needleworker were manufactured at the factory of Mikhail Lomonosov, who was renowned not only as a great scholar but also a talented engineer and an astute entrepreneur. In 1755-1768 his glass factory, located in the vicinity of St. Petersburg, manufactured glass beads, spangles and smalt for mosaics. He produced splendid decorative glass, using local raw materials, original techniques and unique equipment. The Imperial court acquired everything that was made by the factory. When the factory went out of business some things were purchased by private individuals. The material was unique in that it consisted of three layers: the outer layer was transparent, in the middle was a thin layer of colored glass and the interior was covered with brilliant metal which gave the beads a mirror-like sparkle.

O.V. Molchanova

Fig. 41.
"Bridal Party before the Wedding in Toropets"
Artist unknown, late 18th century
Oil on canvas
64.5 x 83.5 cm
State Historical Museum 10060/II-2035

In folk culture of the 18th century, a wedding was one of the traditional holidays celebrated according to ancient local customs. The wedding ceremony in the church was preceded by a ceremonial matchmaking, a presentation of the bride-to-be, an agreement and a farewell to maidenhood, all of which was known as the "prenuptials".

The painting depicts the presentation of the bride-to-be (in a public ceremonial to the groom or his relatives) or a "devishnik" (celebration of the end of maiden life on the eve of the wedding) which takes place in the ancient trading city of Toropets, in the Pskov region (founded in 1016).

In the 18th century the simple Russian population usually wore festive peasant costumes for social occasions. The clothing of the petty bourgeoisie and merchants was famous for its originality, combining elements of European and peasant dress, which was worn with a special elegance. According to legend, dolls representing the women of Toropets were given as gifts to Empress Catherine the Great in connection with the interest at court in folk art during her reign. Emperor Alexander I made a special stop in Toropets during a trip through Russia to admire these rare costumes.

A pyramid shaped kokoshnik (head dress) with a long veil reaching to the ground would be worn by a married woman, decorated with fresh water pearls in the shape of rounded cones. Fans also were used. Young girls and married women could use the veil or fan to cover their faces in public.

The painting obviously portrays a festive table in the house of the bride, who is sitting to the right of the head of the table, her face partially covered with a black shawl. Next to the bride one can see a tiny figure of a girl who looks like a dwarf in her adult clothes. She is "the bride's understudy" who replaces the bride during some of the pre-nuptial ceremonies. All the guests are wearing their best clothes for the occasion and the food being served is primarily sweets. The bridesmaids are sitting on a high bench at the table; their faces covered with fans. On the left the painter depicted some guests in European clothing and, possibly, a matchmaker who is ushering in the groom.

It seems unlikely that the subject of the painting is connected with an actual event: a marriage between a nobleman and a rich middle class girl or a merchant's daughter was very rare at the end of the 18th century. Both sides would try to keep such an arrangement secret. The painting "Bridal Party before the Wedding in Toropets" is a rare genre picture witnessing folk tradition in provincial town life at the end of the 18th century.

N. Perevezentseva

Fig. 42.
Wedding Chest
Early 18th century
Wood (pine), iron, gilding, carving, painting
57 x 45 x 35 cm
State Historical Museum 55412/440

The ornate carving on the chest greatly resembles the carving on the iconostasis of a church or on the Royal Doors. It is obvious that the author was a church wood carver who was given a special commission. The ornamental pattern features ripe grapes in various colors associated with a celebration. It is very likely that the chest was a wedding gift or part of the dowry of a bride.

N. Goncharova

Fig. 43.
Festive Dress of a Woman of the North
Northern Russia,
late 18th - early 19th century

Sarafan
End of the 18th – early 19th century
Length 119 cm, hem width 338 cm
State Historical Museum 49704 B-448 CB -
1424
The sarafan is sewn in fine purple silk giving the effect of moire. Along the slit and the hem the sarafan is decorated with a wide band of golden lace. The thick lining is made of blue canvas, over a thin layer of cotton.

Vest ("Dushegreya")
End of the 18th – early 19th century
Length 40 cm
State Historial Museum 5046 B-544
The dushegreya is a short outer garment
with sleeves which are puffed at the top and

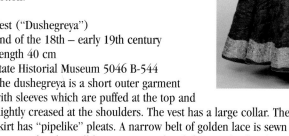

slightly creased at the shoulders. The vest has a large collar. The bodice is detachable. The skirt has "pipelike" pleats. A narrow belt of golden lace is sewn along the waistline and is decorated with small buttons covered with fabric. The floral patterned brocade vest was made in Russian in the second half of the 18th century. The pattern is in the form of small floral bouquets and flowering plant shoots. Golden threaded fringe decorates the edge of the collar and the lapel. The vest is fastened with metal hooks. The lining is quilted cotton.

Blouse
19th century
100 cm in length
State Historical Museum 83200/82 B-1279
The long sleeved white blouse is made of white cotton; its body is made out of homespun canvas. The small pleated collar is decorated with a pattern. The sleeves are adorned with "filet" lacy embroidery.

Necklace
Early 19th century
43 cm in length
State Historical Museum 102206 CH-726
The ornamental necklace is comprised of 16 canvas strips embroidered with particles of mother-of-pearl. It is decorated with 5 large pieces of colored glass strung on galloon braid. The necklace fastens with a metal hook.

Gold Threaded Scarf
Olonets province of Kargopol region, early 20th century
101 x 100 cm
State Historical Museum 33206 D-855
The white calico scarf is embroidered with gold and silver threads and is decorated with gilded fringe and large plant ornamentation in one corner. The scarf is marked
<<A.P.C.>> in white cottom thread embroidery.

L. V. Yefimova

Fig. 44. (above left)
Wooden Mold for Prianiki (gingerbread) in the form of the emblem of the Russian Empire, Russia, late 19th century
Wood, carving, 22.2 x 21.5 x 4.5 cm
State Historical Museum 33749 / 321

Numerous ceremonies in Russian daily life were associated with prianiki. No festive dinner, names-day celebration, wedding, funeral, or any other event could possibly take place without them. According to popular belief prianiki had healing powers and could cure serious diseases.

Special molds with carved patterns were used to create the shaped prianiki. An artist made a drawing of a pattern on a board and then an experienced carver did the rest. Dough for prianiki was pressed into the carved mold and the pattern was shaped. The subjects were highly varied: double-headed eagles, lions, birds, riders, and fish. After they were baked the prianiki were decorated with colored icing and tinsel. They looked like precious enameled objects, and after this final stage they became real works of art.

Fig. 45. (above right)
Molded Prianik in the form of a Sterlet
Tver, late 19th – early 20th century
Preserved dough, 28 cm in diam.
State Historical Museum 51820/3405

Among the most loved and popular subjects for molded prianiki was the sterlet, a common fish of northern waters. Rolled up like a wheel the sterlet would push itself with its tail at the bottom of the river and "roll" across shallow waters when going off to spawn.

N. Goncharova

Fig. 46.
Veliky Ustiug, *Panorama of the City from the Sukhona River*
Vasily K. Berezin, 1795
Oil on canvas
351 x 71.5 cm
State Historical Museum 17026ch K348

Center inscription on banner: "The city of Veliky Ustiug, previously in the former Vologotsk Province."

Inscription in left cartouche with geographical and historical description of the city, the artist's signature and date: "This city was painted by Vasily Berezin, citizen of Ustiug, in 1795".

Inscription on the water: "The Sukhona River from Vologda to Veliky Ustiug is 500 versts." (1 verst = .66 miles)

Inscription in lower right corner where two rivers meet: "Dvina River", "Yug River".

Inscription shown on land at lower right: "Distance from St. Petersburg, 1269 v. – from Moscow, 1000v".

The city of Veliky Ustiug was founded on the left bank of the Sukhona River, a tributary of the Northern Dvina, by settlers from the principality of Rostov-Suzdal in the middle of the 12th century. Until the beginning of the 18th century the city was one of the most important trading centers of Northeast Russia connecting the Muscovite state with the White Sea, the Northern Urals and Siberia. In the center of this panoramic view the ensemble of Cathedral Square can be seen, with the Dormition Cathedral, the first stone cathedral in the north of Russia, built in the 17th century, and the Archbishop's house. Veliky Ustiug is famous for its enamels of the 17th and 18th centuries. (See Cat.No.85, 87)

N. Skorniakova

Fig. 47.
Chest with the portrait of Peter I
Veliky Ustiug, early 18th century
Wood, oak, iron, tempera colors
21 x 45 x 33.5 cm
State Historical Museum 48237 / 8

This type of chest was used by travelers for their money, valuables, and documents, but it was also used as a head support. The lid was slanted and the traveler could put his head on it. To strengthen the chest, it was bound with strips of iron. The chest was decorated with colored paper and inlaid mica and the interior of the lid was colorfully painted.

According to legend, Peter I was often portrayed riding a white horse. His activities were closely connected with the Russian North and in 1693 he visited the city of Archangelsk. He lived there for a short time during the construction of a fortress on the River Dvina. It is quite natural that the visit of such an important guest would inspire the work of local painters. The artist indicates the Emperor not only by his grand posture, but also by his tall figure and the different color of his horse. The Emperor is already in foreign dress. It is a well known fact, that after returning to Moscow from abroad, the tsar shaved his beard, leaving only his mustache, and started to wear Dutch clothing: a short belted caftan, stockings, short boots and a soft hat with a low crown. One can see all these details in the image of Peter on the lid of the chest.

The painter subtly informs us of his negative attitude towards the tsar by portraying the emperor's horse with an enormous phallus. The people did not approve his second marriage with Skavronskaya and felt sorry for his lawful wife Evdokya Lopukhina who was exiled by the tsar. The painter tried to depict Peter's indecent behavior and his promiscuity with all the means at his disposal.

N. Goncharova

Fig. 48.
Shawl
Russia, 1830's
Wool, hand double-face weaving, reversible rug technique
White ground, border of lilac branches, wool fringe
Embroidered mark: " N.M., double-headed eagle and St. George."
Factory of Nadezhda A. Merlina
Ryazan Province, Yegoriev Region, Village of Podryadnikovo
139 x 137 cm
Received by the Museum in 1925
State Historical Museum 55753 D-46

In 1800, Nadezhda Appollonovna Merlina, a Russian landowner, organized the production of colored woolen reversible rugs at her estate in the village of Skorodumovka, Lukoyanov region of Nizhny Novgorod Province. In 1806 her serf factory started manufacturing shawls and scarves. The whole production process was concentrated on the estate. Goat down, fallow deer down, and various natural dyes were bought at the Nizhny Novgorod Fair. Serf craftsmen combed the down with ivory combs and spun the finest yarn. Thirteen grams of yarn was enough to produce 4500 m. of thread. Woolen threads were dyed in various colors and shades. A craftsman called Ivan Pryamikov was in charge of dying threads at the Merlin factory. He obtained "colors of pleasant shades, bright and durable."

The most demanding work was carried out by young serf weavers who had nimble fingers and good eyesight. They worked on small looms and used little wooden bobbins to weave wide and narrow bands, corners, and singe color fabric. Creating the reversible pattern was the most difficult task. Ends of colored threads had to be hidden so that the face and reverse sides of the shawl's patterned edges looked equally clean-cut and neat. Finally all of the details and individually woven sections were assembled into one whole product.

Each item was custom made according to the individual design of an artist. During the 1830-40's, square shaped shawls were in fashion. Square shaped shawls would be folded in half and worn on one's shoulder.

Serf weavers of 14 to 18 years of age could recreate with remarkable accuracy all of the picturesque nuances of complicated floral compositions. This meticulous work was very time-consuming and tedious. At the Merlin estate, 60 weavers working on 24 weaving machines could produce up to 16 large shawls and 19 square scarves and kerchiefs per year.

Reversible hand woven items were highly valued by contemporary consumers.

Shawls and scarves manufactured by the Merlin factory received numerous gold medals at the industrial exhibitions in Moscow and St. Petersburg. Merlina marked the products of her workshop with her initials "N.M." beginning in 1829. In the 1830's she received permission to use the Russia Imperial eagle as a sign of excellent quality.

In 1834, Merlina transferred her factory to the village of Podryadnikov in the Egoryev Region of Ryazan Province.

The products of Merlina's factory were very costly (from 1,000 to 12,000 rubles) and were in demand among the wealthiest aristocratic families and at court.

Merlina displayed her products for the last time at the International Industrial Exposition in London in 1851.

O. G. Gordeyeva

Kvas is a popular fermented beverage, typically made at home in Russian peasant villages or in merchant residences. This original vessel for kvas is in the form of a disk with an opening in the middle. Its spout is extended and curved, and the composition of the handle consists of scalloped scrolls with four legs resembling lion's paws.

The opening in the center of the body of the pitcher is surrounded by a flat relief image of a double-headed eagle and the date 1793. According to tradition a piece of ice wrapped in a cloth was put in the opening to keep the beverage cool.

Vessels such as this, called kvasniks (with solid disks, decorated with architectural motifs, birds, and grass) are characteristic of the majolica objects made in the town of G'zhel, 40 kilometers from Moscow, which is famous for its pottery. G'zhel is the only area in Russia where the Italian type of majolica was manufactured in a wide assortment of items. In addition to kvasniks, pitchers, plates, mugs, inkpots and interesting ethnic figurines were made. The G'zhel majolica was at its peak in the latter part of the 18th century.

T. I. Dulkina

Fig. 49.
Kvasnik (pitcher for traditional Russian fermented beverage)
G'zhel, Moscow Province, 1793
Majolica, polychrome
30 cm in height
State Historical Museum 42491/I fc

Fig. 50.
Snuff Box with Map of the Aleutian Islands
Siberia, mid-19th century
Silver, niello
2.6 x 8.5 x 8.5 cm
State Historical Museum 582/279

Niello is one of the most ancient techniques for decorating precious metals, known even in ancient Egypt. It is a special powder consisting of an alloy of sulfuric silver and other metals, which is used to fill a carved out design on a precious object. After the piece is fired in a kiln furnace and its surface cleaned, the blackened niello outline is so firmly bonded to the metal that it cannot be removed.

The art of niello has a special elegance with great technical possibilities for the decoration of jewelry. It can be used to create various ornamental patterns and scenes, or even graphically reproduce social, historical or religious scenes, inscriptions, etc.

In spite of its wide geographical usage, the art of niello became particularly popular in Russia, where it has been used since the 10th century. In the 16-17th centuries Moscow was the center of the art of niello. However, in the 18th century this art came to be practiced in the new capital of St. Petersburg and from there it spread further to such northern cities as Veliky Ustiug, Vyatka, Vologda, Arkhangel'sk and even as far as Siberia.

The Siberian city of Tobolsk is renowned for the greatest number of silver objects decorated in niello. In the 1770s there was a short-lived but very productive period in the art of niello. It is possible that this was due to the energetic and powerful figure of Governor Denis Chicherin (1763-1781). One can see in the work of Siberian silver craftsmen, images of the Siberian landscape, plans of cities, maps of Siberia and the New World and local hunting scenes. There are some pieces whose shape is very unusual, for instance, a snuffbox made in the form of a wicker tea box, packaged and tied with a rope reminding its owner of foreign trade from Siberia. (Cat.No.126)

Most of the existing silver and niello pieces made in Tobolsk were commissioned by Governor Chicherin and often bear his coat of arms or initials, or even a miniature oil portrait inside the lid of a snuff box. Denis Chicherin was a generous and extravagant man who loved comfort, luxury and beautiful things.

In 1765 he sent to the Empress Catherine II "a parcel containing a description of the Aleutian Islands discovered in 1741-1764." It is possible that the silver snuff-box with niello maps of Siberia and the northeast, the adjacent seas and the "newly-found Aleutians" was commissioned expressly for that occasion.

G. Smorodinova

Fig. 51.
Ethnographic Map of the first Kamchatka
Expedition of Vitus Bering (1725-1740)
Unknown author, mid-18th century
Paper, watercolors, ink
62.0x132.0 cm
State Historical Museum
57025/GO-1882/3

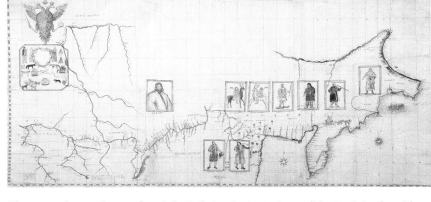

Fig. 52.
Ritual Ball of the Chukchi tribe of
Northeastern Siberia
Chukotka, late 19th century
Seal skin, fragments of seal hair
24 cm in height, 66 cm in diameter
State Historical Museum expedition of
1958.
State Historical Museum 96456/763
Leather-498

Paleoasian people of the Artic Zone (such
as Chukchi, Eskimo, Koryak, and others)
have a well developed system of myths
about the creation of the world. The major
figure of these myths is Raven-the-Creator,
who gave deer and dogs to people, and
who taught them deer breeding, fishing,
sea animal hunting, and dog sleighing. The
Sun, the Moon and the Stars were sewn into
balls and kept by the Evil Spirit. The Raven
stole those balls from the Evil Spirit,
pecked the balls into pieces, and set free
the celestial bodies. Decorated balls are
used in folk rituals welcoming the Sun at
the end of long artic nights and used in
sports games during hunting festivals.

O. G. Gordeyeva

The map embraces the area from Lake Baikal to the Arctic Ocean ("the North Sea") and from the origin of the Irtysh River to the Pacific Ocean ("the Pacific Sea"). The coastline is depicted in a sketchy and fragmentary manner: from the Anabar River to the Kolyma estuary the Arctic Ocean coast line is interrupted. The Yenisei River and its tributaries, the upper Ob, Irtysh, Lena and the river network of the Kamchatka peninsula are depicted in a more detailed manner. The map depicts townships, villages, and winter lodges located on the river networks. There are indications of depth measurements taken in the Anadyr Bay and the Bering Strait along the route of the *St. Gabriel*. There are inscriptions on the map which explain that "The upper part of the Irtysh River along with other rivers and known locations, has been copied from a map drawn by the Poutilov survey engineers; the Yenisei River from the source to the estuary, part of the coast line, the upper part of the Ob River with its tributaries, has been copied from the map, drawn by survey engineer Chichagov"; "Copied from the map, drawn by survey engineer Shatilov" (at Lake Baikal); and "High stone mountains are covered with snow even in the summer time and in many parts they rise up adjacent to the sea, like a steep and high wall" (from the Kamchatka peninsula along the Anadyr Bay and the Chukotka Peninsular.)

Here also are 11 images of the ethnic minorities of Siberia, with inscriptions: *Yakut, Tungus and a Reindeer, Tungus Woman and a Reindeer, Koryak, Kurile Native, Kamchatka Woman, Chukotka Native. Kamchatka Native Riding a Dog Sleigh, Chukotka Natives*. In the upper left corner of the map under the double-headed eagle crowned with three crowns there is a blank cartouche.. Around the cartouche are scenes of the everyday life of the people of Siberia: funeral rites, (the cremation of dead bodies and the consumption of dead bodies by dogs), hunting prey, housing, etc.

Inscription next to the lower cartouche: "No. 18/1753 Siberia."

This map is one of 4 versions of an ethnographic map drawn by the First Kamchatka expedition.

Russia does not have the other three versions of this map. This version however, is unique in comparison to the other maps drawn by the members of the Bering expedition in that it contains depth measurements taken in the Anadyr Bay and the Bering Strait. These measurements are an important feature for those who study Bering's route for they help identify correctly the last leg of the voyage made by the *St. Gabriel* before it changed course and returned to port.

E.D. Markina, A.K. Zaitsev.

55

Fig. 53.
Mast of a River Vessel
Volga region
First half of the 18th century
Wood, carving, tempera colors
345 x 112 x 18 cm
State Historical Museum 40140/4569

The carved circle on top of the mast is not only a decorative element but also an ancient protective image. According to popular belief the sun flies across the sky in a chariot and plunges down into the sea for the night. In this case there is a connection between the two ancient cults of the Sun and of Water.

The radiating face of the Sun is in the center of the disk, surrounded by flat figures vaguely resembling people. They are performing a circular dance. The people in the upper part of the ring are raising their hands, while those on the lower part hold their hands down. The circular dance is a ceremony associated with the cult of the sun. The hands up in the air make a gate through which the sun goes up, and the hands that are down represent the sunset, i.e. change of night and day. Thus, the carved ornamentation of the mast is not only decorative but is also an appeal to various forces in nature, obviously for the protection of the travelers.

N. Goncharova

Fig. 54.
Map of the organization of Russian trade in the
Northern Pacific
St. Petersburg, Academy of Science, 1787
Illuminated engraving
60 x 83.5
State Historical Museum 55709/GO-6196

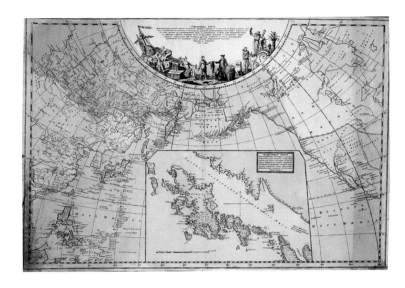

This general map is very useful for viewing expanding Russian trade and seafaring in the Pacific and South Oceans. It shows the adjacent lands and renowned islands lying from the straight separating North America and Asia to the equinox line. Also included are the newly discovered islands of Kyktak, Aphganak and others; the map provides a detailed description of the people who live there and who surrendered to the Russian Empire. It also contains information on villages and various discoveries made by the ships belonging to the Northeast-American Company Golikov and Partners. 1787.

Inset: *A special map of the newly discovered Kyktak and other islands showing the North American coast line, bays harbors, rivers and woods and the location of Russian and other villages and settlements. Depicted by our former partner Gregory Shelikhov.*

An inset narrates the story of proposals on restructuring the Russian fur trade in the Pacific: it portrays a Russian merchant, American Indians and Chinese, and also the image of the god Hermes. There are only two copies of this map known to exist (the second copy is in the Museum of Regional Studies of the city of Temnikov).

For the first time the map indicates the Russian border in America (or rather what Russia claimed as her domain). The official borders were non-existent at the time and no one had made any official claims, so these borders may be regarded as the wishful thinking of the Company. Shelikhov suggested that the border should run along the 55∞ of northern latitude. This was accomplished later, but at that point in time the map indicates that the border runs at about 45∞ northern latitude, which places the Russian domain directly bordering lands claimed by the Spanish. In other words, what is currently the Canadian coast and State of Washington are shown to be under Russian control.

Another important feature of this map that distinguishes it from other maps drawn in the Golikov-Shelikhov Company (for instance, the maps drawn by Shelikhov in 1793 and 1796), is the route from Petropavlovsk to Canton and further as far south as South East Asia. The title of the map includes the description, " ways of expanding Russian trade", thus referring to the project of restructuring the Russian fur trade that was proposed by P.A. Soymonov (politically this project was directed at suppressing British rivalry and establishing Russian domain in Alaska). Under this project the furs purchased by the Company were to be sold in Canton, as China was a major fur market at that time.

V.E. Boulatov

Fig. 55.
Portrait of I. F. Kruzenstern
Unknown artist, 1830
Oil on canvas
94 x 73 cm
State Historical Museum 61843/63

Ivan Feodorovich Kruzenstern (1770-1846) was a seafarer, admiral (since 1841), member of the State Admiralty Department, and member of the Academy of Science of St. Petersburg, Paris, Stockholm, Gettingen and Edinburgh. In 1803-1806 he headed the first Russian voyage around the world on board the ships *Nadezhda* and *Neva* with the participation of Y.F. Lisyansky (the *Neva* captain), F.F. Bellingsauzen and O.E. Kotzebue. They made a mapping survey of the Marquis Islands, the southern part of Sakhalin, part of the Kuriles, and the west coasts of the islands of Hondo (Nippon), Honshu, Hokkaido, and the southern part of Kamchatka. I.F. Kruzenstern used the 1803-1806 round world expedition materials in compiling *The Atlas of the South Sea...* (the southern part of the Pacific) published in 1824-1827 and modified in 1835 and 1838.

A.K. Zaitsev, V.E. Boulatov

Fig. 56.
Vestments of an Orthodox Priest
Podriznik, epitrachilion, sash, nabedrenik,
phelon, poruchi
Pendant cross with chain, panagia with
chain
Russia, late 19th century
Deer skin, leather, and embroidery
State Historical Museum
55114/1401-1408

This is a unique set of vestments made of suede and reindeer fur, used by a priest of the Russian Orthodox Church doing missionary work among the native peoples of Siberia.

Russian missionaries modeled their work on the principles of St. Stephen of Perm who in the 14th century, tried to convert to Christianity the Zyryan people (tribes of Ugro-Finnish origin) who lived in the Perm region. He mastered their language, invented a written Zyryan alphabet and translated basic Biblical and theological books into that language. St. Stephan also built churches, opened new schools and ordained the best of his disciples. The principles established by St. Stephen became the highest ideal of the Russian missionaries in their work of evangelization among the numerous ethnic minorities living in the huge open spaces of Siberia.

The 19th century saw a great number of missionaries who were involved in education and enlightenment, especially Ivan Veniaminov (1797-1879), who began his career as a priest and missionary in the Aleutian Islands. When he retired, his missionary work completed, he had established four large and self-sufficient dioceses: the Aleutians and Alaska, Vladivostok and Kamchatka, the Amur and Blagoveschensk, and Yakutsk and Viluysk. He spent 16 years (1824-1840) working in Russian America. In 1840 he was made bishop, and then archbishop, and was given the name of Innokenty (1840-1868).

In 1868 he was transferred to Moscow where he was appointed Metropolitan and Head of the Russian Orthodox Church. He authored numerous books on theology, religion and education, and scientific chronicles. St. Innokenty is rightly called the Apostle to Siberia and America.

In 1870 Metropolitan Innokenty established an Orthodox Missionary Association in Moscow, which directed all missionary activities of the Russian church. The Association was involved in fund raising throughout Russia to help support priests, open churches, schools, and hospitals; and publish books. The association established diocesan committees in Russian cities and by the early 20th century, 48 committees had been established. The Association membership was more than 15,000 and some of the constituents made very generous donations. The Association took care of 8 missions in Siberia, 13 missions in the European region of Russia and also missions in China and Japan.

Many distinguished Russians sat on the Board of the Association, including the President of Moscow University. In the 1880's G.A. Ivanov, a Privy Counselor, was President of Moscow University. This is important because the deer skin vestments were acquired by the Historical Museum from the Museum of Moscow University in 1923. Unfortunately no documents accompanied the vestments, which might have shed some light on the mystery of their origin. All efforts (in the archives and historical and literary research) have been to no avail. It is obvious that these unique vestments were made for a very special occasion, as their creation required a great deal of love, patience, skill and artful work. Possibly, they were made for the celebration of the 30th anniversary of the Missionary Association, or perhaps, for the celebration of the 300th anniversary of the Romanov dynasty. It is also possible that this event was in some manner connected with Moscow University and its President. Judging by the fur processing technique, the use of multicolored fur inlay and embroidery along the hem of the suede phelon and other indications, it can be concluded that the vestments could have originated in Yakutia or Kamchatka. At the present time it is not possible to attribute them to any particular region. However it seemed appropriate to exhibit them for the first time and to draw public attention to them.

O.G.Gordeyeva

Fig. 57.
Folding Triptych Icon with *The Mother of God, The Saviour and Sts. Sergius, Nicholas, Zosima and Savvati, The Annunciation and Guardian Angel, Sts. Metropolitans Peter, Alexis and Jonah*
Russia
17th century, restored 19th century
Wood, tempera, gilded silver, pearls, rubies, emeralds
17.2 x 23.5
State Historical Museum 74823/10136

A portable folding icon of this type was most commonly used in Russia by travelers since medieval times. The saints represented on the icon would be chosen as patron saints of members of the family. A prayer before an icon would bring peace of mind and a sense of protection to the traveler who might be a long way from any church and often had to face dangerous or hostile forces in nature.

This icon, so richly decorated, would surely have belonged to a noble traveler or perhaps an officer who might have been sent on duty to Siberia or the New World.

Fig. 58.
Mitre of a Bishop
Russia, early 19th century with details from the 17th, 18th and 19th centuries
Gold, silver, pearls, diamonds, sapphires, rubies, emeralds, enamel, velvet, silk
23.2 cm in ht.
State Historical Museum 77319/10821

Fig. 59.
Wedding Crowns
St. Petersburg,
early 19th century
Gilded silver, enamel, brass, velvet
23.5 x 27 x 27 cm
State Historical Museum 68257/8712, 8713

During a Russian Orthodox wedding service, crowns are held over the heads of the bride and groom, symbolizing their new position as "king" and "queen" of their new domain of home and family. There is also a deeper theological meaning of the crowns as symbols of a kind of "martyrdom" or giving up an independent life for a common life "for better or for worse." According to Orthodox understanding, martyr-saints receive a "crown of glory" in the heavenly kingdom.

The use of crowns in the wedding service goes back to Byzantine practice when the bride and groom actually wore crowns, as it is still done in the Greek Church today. In Russia however, the crowns came to be simply held over the heads of the bridal couple as it was believed that only the tsar and his consort could wear a crown.

M. Swezey

Fig. 60.
Icon of *"The Nativity"*
Russian North, 16th century
Wood, tempera colors
91.5 x 61 cm
State Historical Museum 53054/4449

The Nativity of Christ, celebrated on December 25 according to the Gregorian Calendar and on January 7 according to the Julian Calendar, still observed by the Russian Orthodox Church, is one of the twelve major feasts of the Liturgical year.

The traditional representation of the Nativity on Russian icons is permeated with the jubilant spirit of this great Mystery, based on the words of the Christmas Hymn, "Christ is Born! Glorify Him!" Heaven and earth – all of the visible and invisible worlds are called to glorify the new-born Saviour of the world.

Byzantine-Russian iconography in its fullness, is linked with the historical development of the Christian consciousness, and an understanding of the texts of Holy Scripture, which bring into the iconographic representation of concrete events, elements of abstract theology. In the center of the icon, surrounded by a circle of mountains, earthly firmness, one finds the dark opening of the cave. The manger with the new-born swaddled infant is on a dark background, with an ox and an ass, representing people of the outside world looking in. The Mother of God, the main protagonist, is in the center of the composition. But the second scene of the reclining Mother is outside the cave and her pose, turning away from the Infant, has deep meaning that is not seen in the realistic portrayal of these events in Western art. It is an image of the profound silence of contemplation and a deeply pensive Mother of God. In the symbolism of the attributes of a church, the altar represents both the cave and the grave of the Lord.

The cave is surrounded by hills and ledges – the firmness of the earth – on which are positioned all of the participants in this event. All of these witnesses are united in their participation in this great mystery – the deeply contemplative Joseph, the glorifying angels, the Magi, followers of the Star, and the midwives bathing the Infant.

This icon is a monument of the region of Novgorod. Its artistry is distinguished from the spiritual content of its powerful images. There is simplicity along with the inherent greatness, in the rhythm of the placement of the figures in the composition, the ornamentation of the hills, the folds of the clothing and the silhouettes, and in the bold use of colors, the blue of the water, the font, the blank spaces and the red in the pallet. There is the characteristic combination of three-dimensional figures and the flat spaciousness of the composition, a density with aquarelle transparency. The asceticism is tempered by the emotional expression. The mastery of the iconographer is not spent on details (hands, for instance, are covered, feet are hidden) but on the extremely expressive "faces" of the horses, the shepherds and the animals of the stable, which are so vivacious in contrast to the other figures, sunk in pensive contemplation. The pink skin tones, the graceful outlines of the features and the classical iconographic style are reminiscent of the culture of the previous century, but the prevalence of line and the use of silhouette in the artistic repertoire, all point to the mature style of the 16th century.

Russians sought to grasp the miraculous mystery of the Birth of Christ not just in Church circles, but also in folklore and in everyday life. Carols sung on Christmas Eve are also about the Magi, the shepherds and the righteous Joseph. The "acting out" of the events of Christmas in the creche or manger scene, provided the basis for the originality of the Slavic theatre. In Russia, the custom of a live Christmas tree decorated with ornaments and presents for children in honor of the gifts presented by the Magi to the Infant Jesus, is beloved by all.

L. Kornukova

The Feast of the Presentation of the Virgin in the Temple is one of the twelve major feasts of the Liturgical year, celebrated on November 21 (December 4 on the Julian Calendar still used in the Russian Orthodox Church).

The life of the Virgin Mary is surrounded by profound mystery and the circumstances of this event in her childhood, with its deep inner meaning, is known only in the tradition of the Church.

The righteous Joachim and Anna, parents of the Virgin Mary, prayed for an end to their barren state, promising to dedicate a child born to them to the service of God. When Mary turned three, her parents fulfilled their vow. Gathering their family and friends and with their daughter dressed in her best clothing, Joachim and Anna set off for the Temple in Jerusalem, singing sacred hymns and carrying lighted tapers. The High Priest met them at the entrance. A stairway of 15 steps led into the Temple. Mary, as soon as she overcame the first step, quickly rose to the top. Then the High Priest, Zachariah, took the Holy Virgin into the Holy of Holies, usually entered only once a year by the priest bearing cleansing blood from the sacrifice. The infant, having crossed the secret threshold, prepared to become "a living temple". For 12 years, until the age of puberty when tradition decreed that she must leave the Temple, Mary lived like a "dove". Her food was brought by an angel.

The theological meaning of the Feast of the Presentation in the Temple is the blessing of God to mankind in this prediction of the coming of Christ and the beginning of salvation. The hymns of this Feast Day service retell the story of Mary's entrance into the temple built by human hands where God dwelt invisibly and incomprehensibly. There she would become the "corporeal receptacle of the incorporeal God", a living temple in which God would become incarnate for the salvation of mankind. In this connection the Nativity hymn "Christ is born, glorify Him" is sung during the Matins of this Feast.

The source of this icon type is found in Byzantine and ancient Russian art, which goes back to the 11th century, from which time it has remained basically unchanged. The iconographer has strictly followed tradition.

The style of this icon, created by a master of the Russian North, seems to belong to the Vologda school. This is evident in the Russification of the broad, round-eyed, large-lipped, oval shaped faces, the chocolate "ochres", the monochrome tonal color and the indeterminate drawing of details. This is compensated by the expression of human feeling. The Vologda school was influenced by the great Dionysius who worked in that region at the end of the 15th and the beginning of the 16th century. The work of the disciples of this school is distinguished by a special state of balance and smooth motion, concluding in the majestic rhythm of the ceremonial processions. The school of this genius iconographer is characterized by daring diagonal line, the careful construction of architectural detail and special use of the color white, making the icon part of a fresco. The elongated proportions, the complex linear structure, measured rhythms as in a dance, the transparent quality of the colors all create an impression of unearthly beauty and spiritual delight. These details make the figure of Mary, in its humble submissiveness stretching out her little pitcher-shaped palms to the priest Zachariah and her Guardian Angel, all the more expessive.

L. Kornukova

Fig. 61.
Icon of *"The Presentation of the Virgin in the Temple"*
Vologda, early 16th century
Wood, tempera colors
82 x 61.5 cm
State Historical Museum 108940/3721

Fig. 62.
Illuminated Manuscript of the
"Apocalypse"
Copy by Fedor Mitelkov, 1859,
of manuscript of Bishop Andrew of
Caesaria (6th century)
with 72 miniatures in tempera and gold
Paper, ink, cinnabar, tempera colors,
wood, leather, copper, gilding
37 x 23 x 6 cm
State Historical Museum 59596/3507

The Apocalypse is the last book of the New Testament where, in symbolic visions, the Apostle John the Theologian represents the Second Coming of Christ, the final battle with the forces of evil and the approaching Kingdom of Heaven. There have been numerous illustrations of the Apocalypse, but one of the most popular was that of Andrew, Bishop of Ceasaria in the 6th century. The *Apocalypse with Illustrations* was translated into Russian long before Tatar rule. Its numerous illustrations were known since the 16th century. The Old Believer community particularly valued the *Apocalypse with Illustrations* and this example originated there.

This manuscript was written in 1859 by Fedor Mitelkov. He has tried to imitate the special style of script of the 16th century. The date of this manuscript and the name of the scribe, written into the epilogue to the Apocalypse in a complicated system of coded lettering, was learned only when that was decoded. It is possible that Fedor Mitelkov was also the author of the illustrations that are done in a very individualized style like the pattern of the manuscript, although the book follows ancient traditions. In the composition of the miniatures, Mitelkov has followed the canons of ancient Russian icon painting.

The page that opens Chapter 45 shows the seven angels sent to earth with chalices of God's wrath. The angels receiving the chalices from God the Father, the Son and the Holy Spirit (as represented on the ancient Russian icon of the New Testament Trinity) can be seen in the upper part of the composition. Below that, can be seen the three angels with harps standing on the surface of a "glass sea" in the midst of fire. According to the interpretation they are symbols of the purity of the devout, enlightened by the fire of God's reason. The harps are symbols of spiritual harmony. The heading and beginning letter of the text on the adjoining page are done in transparent color with the use of stylized vegetation motifs.

E.I. Serebryakova

Fig. 63.
*Triumphant Procession of Emperor
Alexander II across Ivanov Square of the
Moscow Kremlin after the coronation in
the Uspensky Cathedral, 1856*
Gustav Schwartz, circa 1856
Oil on canvas
71 x 109 cm
State Historical Museum 87870/K47

Fig. 65.
Equestrian Harness and Headgear made
for the Coronation of Alexander II
St. Petersburg, Valter and Cox, 1857
Bronze, silver, brass, leather, velvet, gold
thread, horse hair, gilding, needlework
Headgear: bridle and blinders, 140 cm in
length
Saddle with fastening belts: 209 cm in
length, 13 cm in width
State Historical Museum 63315/3633

The German painter G. Shwartz worked in Russia for more than 20 years, mainly on commissions of Nicholas I. He specialized in battle scenes, military parades and maneuvers. In 1856 he completed a set of three pictures devoted to the coronation of the new Russian Emperor Alexander II.

For a long time these pictures were kept in the collection of the Petrovsky Palace in Moscow and in the 1920's they were transferred to the Historical Museum.

The Coronation of Alexander II took place on August 26, 1856. The Russian Emperors, like their predecessors the Grand Princes and Tsars of Moscow, were crowned in the Uspensky Cathedral of the Moscow Kremlin. The coronation ceremony was elaborated in great detail in the 18th century. On the eve of the ceremony temporary wooden pavilions were erected in the Kremlin for viewers. They were made in the style of ancient Russian houses. On the Kremlin walls, towers, and the Ivan Veliky Bell Tower special wooden scaffolding was built for viewing the fireworks. A special wooden platform decorated with scarlet cloth was constructed on the Cathedral and Ivanov squares. The platform connected the palace with the main cathedrals for the ceremonial procession of the emperor and his entourage.

The painting portrays Ivanov Square after the coronation when the Emperor had already left the Uspensky Cathedral. Traditionally, the ceremony was accompanied by a 101 gun salute and the ringing of bells in all of the Moscow churches. In the center of the composition is the Ivan Veliky Bell Tower. To the right one can see the ensemble of the ancient Chudov monastery (founded in the 14th century) and the facade of the Small Nikolaevsky Palace, where Grand Duke Alexander Nikolaevich, the future Emperor Alexander II was born in 1818.

This ceremonial equestrian gear consisting of a decorative saddle and bridle with blinders is one of a set made for a tandem of six horses for the coronation of Alexander II which took place on August 26, 1856. Tandem harness was introduced in Russia during the reign of Catherine II and was especially popular in the late 18th and early 19th centuries. In a tandem, harnessed horses follow each other in line either singly or in pairs.

For the coronation of Alexander II, Court workshops and private manufacturers made 27 gilded carriages, 5 phaetons and blinders for 196 horses for the gala procession. The Court stables and private stud farms provided 462 riding horses for the ceremony. 281 men dressed in gala uniforms were responsible for the harnessed and riding horses. Splendid Danish horses were used for the tandems.

I.N. Paltusova

Fig. 64.
Portrait of Alexander II on a horse
N.E. Sverchkov, 1871
Oil on canvas
74 x 98 cm

Fig. 66.
The Moscow Kremlin
Peter P. Vereschagin, 1868
Oil on canvas
50 x 68 cm
State Historical Museum 701156/K240

P.P. Vereschagin, academician and well-known painter of landscapes, was born in the city of Perm into a family of many generations of icon painters. He painted mainly city landscapes. In 1868 the Petersburg Art Academy awarded him the title of "Painter of the 1st Rank" for his works: "A Flea Market in Moscow" and "The Moscow Kremlin ".

The Kremlin ensemble is shown from across the Moscow River, on the Sofia embankment near the Large Stone Bridge.

N. Skorniakova

Moscow, first mentioned in the chronicles in 1147, is one of the most ancient cities of Russia. A small town in the 14th and 15th centuries, Moscow became the center of a unified Russian state by the 16th century because of its geographical position and the role of the Moscow princes in the liberation of Russia from the Tatars. In the 16th century, Moscow surpassed the largest cities of Europe in size and population. The Kremlin, with its fortress walls of red brick and white stone cathedrals with golden cupolas, was the residence of the Moscow Princes and Tsars until the 18th century when Peter the Great moved the capital to his new city of St. Petersburg. Moscow retained its importance, however, as the political, economic and cultural center of Russia. The coronations of all the emperors took place in Moscow, which has always been the spiritual center of Russia, with more than 450 churches by the end of the 19th century.

N.Kargapolova

The bodice is made of pink and purple velvet with a white satin insert in the middle. The dress has long loose hanging sleeves decorated with swan fur. The skirt is made of white satin with a detachable train made of purple and pink velvet. The bodice, sleeves, center of the skirt, and edges of the train are decorated with Russian-made gold and silver lace.

The dress is comprised of three components: purple pink velvet and white satin bodice, embroidered white satin skirt, and a detachable train made of the same velvet, which is almost 3 meters long. The bodice is tightly fitting with a lining containing the so-called "bones", thin flexible whalebone plates that were sewn into the bodice using standard tailoring techniques of the 19th century. The cut and style of the dress relates to the ceremonial occasions for which it had been made – low decoleté , long and wide folding sleeves, rich decoration in the front. The edges of the sleeves are decorated with thin strips of swan fur. The purple pink velvet train on a belt is attached at the waist. The rim of the train is decorated with gold and silver lace. The lace ornamentation consists of meandering ribbons intertwined with ivy garlands and rococo cartouches with charming floral bouquets. Bunches of cane with long fragile leaves stand out among the flowers in this pattern.

It is difficult to determine where the lace was made. It seems that patterns of this kind should originate from Western Europe, since the centers of lacemaking at that time were located in Belgium and France, and Spain was famous for its gold and silver thread making. Nevertheless, Russia could also be the origin of this lacework due to the long tradition of weaving gold and silver lace. On the petticoat lining there is a white ribbon with a very clear black ink inscription: "E.G. Alexeyeva No.3". This must be a mark of a shop, which had supplied the tailoring firm with braids, ribbons, threads, and other sewing accessories.

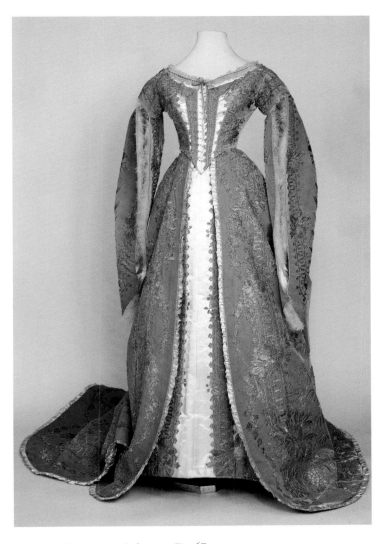

Fig. 67.
Court dress
Russia, 1866
Belonged to Grand Duchess Maria Fedorovna, wife of the future Emperor Alexander III
Velvet, lace, satin, swan fur, embroidery of gold and silver thread
Bodice length: 30 cm, skirt length: 106 cm, train: 296 cm
State Historical Museum 766669/B372

Making this dress required a very slender, special mannequin. Obviously it was made for a very young lady, Princess Dagmar of Denmark, at the time of her engagement to Grand Duke Alexander Alexandrowich, the heir to the Russian throne. She came to Russia on the eve of her wedding ceremony – in the summer or fall of 1866. The Princess, who had just lived through a terrible personal tragedy, was still beautiful and charming. A petite woman with large expressive gray eyes and auburn hair, she had won the heart of the Russian heir to the throne, who was himself, a very imposing young man.

One can imagine that unknown Russian seamstresses made this dress for the arrival of a noble-born bride to Russia. The choice of color for this dress is quite remarkable: the pastel purple-pink velvet must have reminded Dagmar of heather. In spring its abundant flowers covered the dunes and fields of her homeland like a carpet. The velvet used for the princess's dress has a touch of silver, which goes remarkably well with the subdued glitter of silver lace. The purple color is a symbol of friendship, loyalty, and remembrance. The pink symbolizes pining for love.

The Russian craftsmen who created this dress – an outstanding work of art – wanted to include details which would remind the future Russian Empress of her beautiful Motherland.

T. S. Alyoshina

65

Fig. 69.
Portrait Badge with Alexander II and
Alexander III
Russia, 1881
Leopold Seltigen, Court Jeweler
Gold, silver, paste, paper, tempera colors
8.4 x 5 cm
State Historical Museum 10525/22560

This rare Imperial award was given to
Prince A.M. Gorchakov, Russia's Minister
of Foreign Affairs from 1856 - 1882, in
1881 shortly before his retirement. It
bears the images of the two Emperors
whom he served, Alexander II and
Alexander III. Prince Gorchakov was
responsible for many of Russia's important
foreign policy decisions, including the sale
of Alaska to the United States in 1867, a
decision fully supported by Alexander II.
The badge was acquired by the State
Historical Museum in 1905 from the
Schukin collection.

M. Swezey

Ed. Note: Historical information on this
Portrait Badge was generously provided by
Ulla Tillander- Godenhielm, Historian of
Russian Jewelry, and Marvin Lyons, Russian
Military Historian.

Fig. 68.
Uniform of a high-ranking courtier
Russia, late 19th – early 20th century
Broadcloth, gold thread, spangles, silk
embroidery
90 cm in length
State Historical Museum 57442/b841

The coat is made of black broadcloth with a red broadcloth collar and cuffs. Front flaps, tails,
seams of the sleeves and back, the collar and cuffs are all decorated with gold thread, pearls, and
spangles. The pattern is comprised of plant elements – palmettos and brushes. There are nine
gilded buttons with the State insignia in the front. Cuffs and flaps have two gilded buttons each with
the State insignia. The coat is fastened with five coconut buttons. White silk lining.

This coat is a sample of the dress uniform of high-ranking courtiers in the late 19th and early
20th century. It was worn with white broadcloth trousers (Cat.No.227) and a black hat embroidered with gold thread and decorated with ostrich feathers. (Cat.No.228)

This type of uniform was introduced in 1834 and was used until 1917. The cut of coats slightly changed in accordance with the fashion of the time. Such a dress coat would be worn only on
certain occasions such as Christmas day, the names-days of the Emperor or Empress, during the
coronation or by special order of the Emperor.

T. S. Alyoshina

This service is decorated with figures dressed in the style of medieval Moscow, characteristic of the revival of interest in Old Russia that took place at the end of the 19th and beginning of the 20th century. The so-called Russian Style is the last "grand" national style of the 20th century, centered in Moscow. With its rich historical past as the source, Moscow experienced a cultural renaissance during this brief period in which creative artists in all mediums, and especially goldsmiths and jewelers, combined traditional stylistic elements in a modern perspective. The resulting national style was quite distinct from the more Europeanized style of St. Petersburg.

The Russian Style began with the revival of the art of Old Russia in efforts to recreate ancient items with ornamentation of that time. It became fashionable to decorate objects with views of Russian cities, historical monuments, and portrayals of different events in Russian history, demonstrating love for the motherland and for one's native city. At the same time, objects in imitation of utensils used by common people also came to be made. They were often made in silver in imitation of wood, bark, wicker, etc. (See "Biscuit Dish", Cat.No.257).

The appearance of large Moscow firms, such as Ovchinnikov, Khlebnikov and Kurliukov who were suppliers to the Imperial Court and many royal houses of Europe, served to emphasize the importance of the Moscow school. Impressed by the beauty of the Russian art that had been forgotten and suppressed for almost two centuries in efforts to imitate Western European forms, the Moscow jewelers re-established the Russian Style in their work.

G. Smorodinova

Fig. 70.
Coffee and tea service in the Russian style
Moscow, 1908-1917, Firm of O. Kurliukov
10 pieces: teapot, coffee pot, jam dish, sugar bowl, biscuit dish, spoon for lemon, sugar scoop, sugar tongs, teaspoon, coffee spoon
Silver, enamel, mother-of-pearl
State Historical Museum
95197/14708-17, 1427

Fig. 71.
Desk set
Moscow, 1883, Firm of P. Ovchinnikov
5 pieces: inkwell, saucer, pen, 2 candlesticks
Gilded silver, enamel
Inkwell: 16 x 11.5 x 11.5 cm; saucer, 20.7 cm in diam.; pen: 16.3 cm in length
Candlesticks: 13.9 x 8 x 8 cm
State Historical Museum 27062/9187

The firm of P. Ovchinnikov became the most famous of the Moscow jewelers working in the Russian Style. The life of this prominent entrepreneur and skillful businessman, who founded one of the best jewelry schools in Russia, developed in a most uncommon way. Despite being a former serf of Prince Volkonsky, he became a leader of the Russian Style in art, thanks to his artistic talent (he modeled many pieces of jewelry) as well as his talent as a businessman. P. Ovchinnikov's collection of precious objets d'art won the highest awards of the Moscow 1865 Exposition — Grand Duke Alexander Alexandrovich (the future Tsar Alexander III) awarded Ovchinnikov the title of Court Supplier and a gold medal for "perfection of the national style, intricacy of forms, and nobility of composition." Since that time, his firm became a major participant in national and world expositions, admired by the public and the press, receiving numerous awards.

Works by Ovchinnikov from the 1870s – 1890s demonstrate remarkable beauty and richness in traditional Russian enamel patterns, showing an infinite number of ways to decorate objets d'art. Ornamentation taken from hand-written manuscripts and etchings from the "Antiquities of the Russian State" - a series of illustrated publications on ancient Russian art - were used to decorate a variety of objects, such as icon covers, frames of folding icons, liturgical vessels, tableware, caskets, folders for stationary, etc.

The Renaissance of the art of enamel became possible thanks to a synthesis of research by Russian art scholars, the artistic talent of painters and sculptors, and the genius of the artist and businessman P. Ovchinnikov. He applied the artistic heritage of the past to contemporary silver and gold work, thereby creating original objets d'art that met the design requirements and purpose of contemporary times.

This desk set belonged to the Russian writer Ivan Goncharov, who participated in the voyage of the Putiatin Mission to Japan.

G. Smorodinov

67

Fig. 72.
"Cockerel" wine set
Moscow, 1875-1885
Firm of I. Khlebnikov
7 pieces: carafe, tray, 5 charkas
Silver, enamel
Tray: 48.9 x 39.4; carafe: 38.5 x 31 x 18;
charkas: 6.5 x 9.7 x 6 cm
State Historical Museum 99834/16234-40

The firm of Khlebnikov also made a significant contribution to the development of the national forms in silver and gold work. His name became known to the world after he took part in the World Exposition in Vienna in 1873, where the showcase demonstrating his art attracted the "serious attention of experts" and won two medals. At that exposition he displayed a very carefully selected and diverse collection of pieces in the Russian Style. Frames for folding icons decorated with enamel, which were "breathing with antiquity", won serious recognition of the art experts at the exhibit. He surprised everyone with the original form of a samovar with handles in the shape of a cockerel's head with feet in the form of claws and a tea service to go with it.

The "Cockerel" wine set made in 1875-1884, consists of a cockerel shaped carafe with charkas in the form of chickens. It is decorated with enameled floral ornamentation. This silver masterpiece is marked by wonderful plasticity in expressing the image of a popular folk bird and brilliant enamel décor imitating wooden folk art, all done in silver in the Russian Style. Khlebnikov was widely acclaimed for his enamel work.

G. Smorodinova

Fig.73.
Pieces from the dessert service of Grand
Duke Konstantin Nikolaevich
St. Petersburg, Imperial Porcelain Factory,
1848 Artist, F.G. Solntsev
Porcelain, gilding, painting, guilloche
Wine cooler: 20.5 cm;
cup and saucer: 11.2 x 17.3;
dessert plate: 22.5 cm in diam.
Mark in underglaze blue of the crowned
monogram, "H I" for Nicholas I
State Historical Museum
62549/3332, 3329

The service was commissioned for the wedding of the Grand Duke Konstantin Nikolaevich (1827-1892), the second son of the Emperor Nicholas I, and the Grand Duchess Alexandra Iosiphovna (1830-1911), the daughter of the Duke of Saxe-Altenburg.

The service was made at the Imperial Porcelain Factory in 1848-1852 and included dinner and dessert sets, as well as a tea set. Based on the number of later additions to the service that were manufactured at the factory of the Brothers Kornilovs in St. Petersburg, it is apparent that the service had been used throughout the 19th century.

This service is one of the first examples of the so-called "Russian Byzantine Style" in the decorative and applied arts. It was designed by F. G. Solntsev (1801-1892) in 1847-48, who as a member of an Imperial commission, was in charge of the restoration of buildings of the Moscow Kremlin (1836). He designed the interiors of the reconstructed Grand Kremlin Palace (1837-1840) and also designed the forms and décor of the Kremlin Porcelain Service. He collected, copied, and published images of the treasures belonging to the Russian tsars and created drawings of ornamentation in the "Russian-Byzantine Style" in the 1840s. The service of the Grand Duke Konstantin Nikolaevich is one of the best examples of the original works by F. G. Solntsev.

The service's décor includes cartouches with the monogram of the Grand Duke Konstantin Nikolayevich ("ВККН") and the Russian double-headed eagle. In the decoration of the service, F. G. Solntsev used the style of Near Eastern as well as ancient Russian enamels that were kept in the Armoury Chamber of the Moscow Kremlin and were used at the Russian Court. The architecture and interior style of the era of Tsar Alexei Mikhailovich (1629-1676, ruling from 1645) were considered to be genuinely Russian. Russian artists employed a relatively simple method of reviving the Russian style which can be called "archaeological". Exact copies of individual elements of the style of the era of Alexei Mikhailovich were made with different materials or were reproduced in other kinds of art. These elements were highly prized among artists for their historical authenticity. In the décor of the service of the Grand Duke Konstantin Nikolaevich such exact copies can be seen in the figurines mounted on the lids of objects. They take the shape of the helmet of Alexei Mikhailovich. The helmet was made in Iran in the 16th century and belonged to Prince F. I. Mstislavsky. It was taken over by the Treasury in 1622 (currently it is in the collection of the Armoury Chamber of the Moscow Kremlin). The artist chose a silhouette of this ancient oriental warrior's helmet not only for its stylistic value, but also for its historical significance - it used to belong to the Russian Tsar. Solntsev published a drawing of this helmet in his multi-volume edition of the "Antiquities of the Russian State" (Moscow, 1853, chap. III, book I, No.15-16).

M. A. Bubchikova

Fig. 74.
Photograph of Grand Duke
Konstantin Nikolaevich
Yalta, circa 1880, F. Orlov
21.5 x 13.9 cm
State Historical Museum 95171/VI 7796

Grand Duke Konstantine was a supporter of the eventual sale of Alaska to the United States. (See the Notes of Grand Duke Konstantin to Prince Gorchakov on the activities of the Russian-American Company and the necessity of changing its statutes. Cat. No. 270)

Fig. 75.
Tray with winter scene *"Sliding Hills on the Neglinka River in the Moscow Kremlin during Maslenitsa"*
Russia, early 19th century
From a design by Delabart 1794
Iron, lacquer, painting.
75.5 x 55 x 4,5
State Historical Museum 17650 zh.3988

Maslenitsa, the week before the beginning of Great Lent, (Mardi Gras as it is known in the West) was a most festive Slavonic holiday, celebrating the victory of light and warmth over winter. People amused themselves for the entire week. Each day of Maslenitsa had its own name. Each morning children came out to build snow hills; sometimes clashes developed ending in fistfights. At the end of the holiday people went around the town in sleighs singing and carrying dolls in effigy.

Usually many preparations were made for the first day of Maslenitsa: large hammocks were constructed, tents and tables were erected containing all sorts of sweets. As a rule, Muscovites celebrated Maslenitsa at the gates of Red Square. Beginning on the first day of Maslenitsa, they baked bliny, (special yeast pancakes), a symbol of the sun. On the second day, they would begin to toboggan. In an earlier era the people would carry a pole on a sleigh with a wheel attached, symbolizing the sun.

Favorite spots in Moscow for celebration were the embankments of the Moscow River and the Neglinka River. Many tents and huts of all shapes and sizes were erected along the riverbanks selling all kinds of food. The entire week peddlers walked around offering bliny, nuts, prianiki, and various drinks.

The tray features a painting designed by Delabart and engraved by G.L. Lori. It is a holiday scene viewed from the Trinity Bridge across the Neglinka River and up to the Voskresensky Gate at Kitai-Gorod. On the right is located the Arsenal, while on the left one can see the Trading Rows along the bank of the Neglinka.

L.N. Goncharova

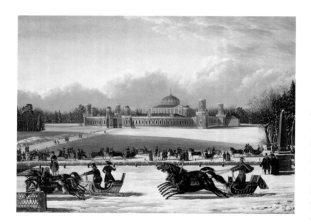

Fig. 76.
Winter Races at the Petrovsky Palace on the outskirts of Moscow
A.A. Golitsyn, 1848
Oil on canvas
66 x 103
State Historical Museum 42567/K258

A.A. Golitsyn was an amateur painter of the ancient family of Golitsyn princes. It appears that besides painting, the artist was also interested in horse racing, especially the sleigh races of the famous Russian troikas. Sleigh racing became widely popular in Moscow at the end of the 18th century as a result of the influence of the well-known Count A.G. Orlov-Chesmensky. It was in his stables that a new line of racehorses was bred, which became known as the Orlov trotter. This kind of winter amusement was popular among all people of the capital from the highest aristocracy to simple people. In the middle of the 19th century races usually took place on the side roads of the Petersburg highway at the Petrovsky Palace, designed by the renowned Moscow architect M.F. Kazakov and commissioned by Empress Catherine the Great in 1775-1782. It was located three versts (2 miles) from the Tver Gate and was under the administration of the palace. In the 1830s the grove around the palace was turned into a park and until the end of the century Petrovsky Park was a favorite place for Muscovites to walk. During the winter it was especially popular for horseback riding and sleigh racing.

N. Skorniakova

Fig. 77.
Folder with an address from American residents of Moscow to V. A. Dolgorukoff, Governor General of Moscow on the occasion of the 25th anniversary of his Governorship
August 31, 1890
Leather, wood, copper, etching, watercolors
48.0 x 37.5
State Historical Museum
91420 kp 9357 1-2

The text of the address:

"*His Excellency, Prince Vladimir Dolgorukoff, Governor General of Moscow.*

Your Excellency,

The United States citizens residing in Moscow, present unto your Excellency their hearty congratulations on the 25th anniversary of your Excellency's tenure of the High Office you have so felicitously administered, and devoutly pray that your Excellency may so continue, in enjoyment of all the blessings of Providence for many years to come.

Moscow, August 31, 1890."

L. A. Dementyeva

Unseen Treasures: Imperial Russia and the New World

Checklist of objects

From the Russian State Historical Museum, Moscow

St. Petersburg and the Imperial Court

1. Silver sculpture, *Peter I on his Botik*
   Model by Mark Antokolsky
   Base by the firm of Falise
   Paris
   1891-1896
   69 x 85 x 45 cm

2. *St. Petersburg and the "Bronze Horseman" monument to Peter I*
   Lithograph, artist unknown
   circa 1820
   30.2 x 46.8 cm

3. *Portrait of Peter I*
   Unknown artist, from the original by I.N. Nikitin
   Oil on canvas
   2nd half of the 18th century
   78.5 x 62 cm

4. Kovsh presented by Peter I to A. Elyseev
   Moscow, 1696
   Silver
   10.5 x 26.4 x 17.9 cm

5. *Panorama of St. Petersburg with a view of the Peter and Paul Fortress*
   Engraving by E.G. Vinogradov from the original by M.I.Mahaev,
   1753
   57 x 79,2 cm

6. Table of the Era of Peter I
   Russia, early 18th century
   Linden wood, carving
   75 x 58 x 36 cm

7. Chair of the Era of Peter I
   Russia, early 18th century
   Wood, fabric, carving
   101 x 55 x 51 cm

8. Tumbler with inscription, *"Vive Tsar Peter Alexeevich"* and the double-headed eagle
   St. Petersburg, 1710
   Yamburg Factory
   Glass, etching

9. Panel from a Door with Decoration on Two Sides, one of a pair: 1) a landscape, 2) Biblical subject from the life of Saul
   Russia, early 18th century
   Wood, tempera
   62 x 69 cm

10. Panel from a Door with Decoration on Two Sides, one of a pair: 1) mountain landscape 2) Biblical subject Jonah and the whale
    Russia, early 18th century
    Wood, tempera
    62 x 69 cm

11. Box with a Medal of the signing of the Treaty of Niestadt in 1721
    Russia, early 18th century
    Silver
    5.1 x 5.1 x 5.1 cm

Checklist of Objects

12. Masquerade Sleigh decorated with "Minerva"
late18th century
Wood, iron, leather, velvet, galloon trim, gilding
312 x 120 x 186 cm

Adorning the sleigh is the figure of Minerva, Roman goddess of wisdom, adopted by Catherine as a symbol of her public image. The sleigh was used by Catherine II in a staged masquerade procession as part of her coronation festivities.

13. *Portrait of Catherine II*
K.L.I. Khristinek from the original by F.S. Rokotov
1780
Oil on canvas
83.5 x 61 cm

14. *Portrait of Catherine II in Russian Costume*
Unknown artist from the original by S. Torelli
Late 18th century
Oil on canvas
68 x 51.2 cm

15. Allegorical painting, *Catherine II traveling through her Realm in 1787*
Unknown artist from the original by F. de Maise
1796
Oil on canvas
61.5 x 71.5 cm

16. Folding Table
Western Europe
mid-18th century
Inlaid wood, carving
79.5 x 112 x 56 cm

17. Gloves of Catherine II
Western Europe
mid-18th century
White kid
25 cm in length

18. Two Oblong Game Markers used by Catherine II
St. Petersburg,
late 18th century
Gold
5.4 x 1 cm

19. Two Round Game Markers used by Catherine II
St. Petersburg,
late 18th century
Gold
2.5 cm in diam.

20. Case for Eyeglasses of Catherine II
St. Petersburg,
late18th century
Silver, gold, enamel, velvet
Inscription
3.1 x 14.4 x 6.2 cm

21. Portable Vessel for the Reserved Eucharist
Moscow, 1764
Silver gilt, enamel
Made for the Church of St. Catherine in Moscow, built by order of Catherine II.
23 x 15.4 x 6 cm

22. *Portrait of Catherine R. Dashkova*
Engraving from the original by Levitsky
After 1784
21.4 x 14.2 cm

An associate of Catherine II and member of the American Philosophical Society. She met Benjamin Franklin with whom she corresponded. President of the Russian Academy of Sciences.

23. *Portrait of G.A. Potemkin*
Engraving from the original by I. Lampi
1789
38.8 x 28.3 cm

In the opinion of several researchers it was this all-powerful lover of Catherine II who influenced her refusal to allow the grandiose plan of Shelikov and Golikov for North America and her decision to leave to "the American people their own destiny".

24. *Portrait of Dmitry M. Golitsyn*
Engraving from the original by F.G. Drew
Late 18th century
50.4 x 37.8 cm

25. *View of the Arch of the General Staff Buildings, Palace Square, St. Petersburg*
K.P. Begrov
Lithograph, 1822
46.5 x75 cm

26. Triptych Icon with the *Mother of God, Saviour and Sts. Sergius, Nicholas, Zosima and Savvati, the Annunciation and Guardian Angel, Sts.Metropolitans Peter, Alexis and Jonah*
Russia, 17th century
Wood, tempera, silver, pearls, rubies and emeralds
17.2 x 23.5 cm

27. Seal
Tula, early 19th century
Steel, polishing and burnishing
7.5 x 5.5 cm

28. Snuff-box with a portrait of Catherine II
Veliky Ustiug, 1787
Master, Ivan Zhilin
Gilded silver, niello
3.5 x 10.4 x 10.4 cm

29. Kovsh presented by Catherine II to the merchant A.B. Zubkov
Moscow, 1774
Gilded silver
29.5 x 40 x 18.5 cm

30-31.
Medals presented by Catherine II "For Useful Work for Society"
St. Petersburg,
late 18th century
Gold
3.4 x 3.4 cm

32. Presentation Ring with Portrait of Catherine II
Russia, late 18th – early 19th century
Gold, silver, amethyst
2.8 x 2.5 x 2.5 cm

33. Candlestick
Tula, late 18th century
Faceted steel, gilded bronze
19 x 12.5 x 12.5 cm

34. Candle snuffer
Tula, late 18th century
5 x 20 x 5.3 cm

35. Inkwell with the bust of Athena
St. Petersburg,
late 18th century
Gilded bronze, amethyst
17.5 x 13 x 13 cm

36. *Portrait of A.A. Bezborodko*
Unknown artist, from the original by I.B. Lampi,
Circa 1790
Oil on canvas
72 x 57 cm

37. Goblet with portraits of Peter I, Elizabeth Petrovna and Catherine II
Russia, late 18th century
Silver, coconut shell
28.5 cm in ht.

38. *Portrait of Paul I*
P.P. Remezov, 1799, from the original by Y.L. Voille
Oil on canvas
76 x 58 cm

39. Signet ring given by Paul I
St. Petersburg, 1796-1801
Gold, diamonds, enamel
1.3 x 2.5 x 2.5 cm

40. *Portrait of Alexander I*
George Dawe
St. Petersburg, 1825
Oil on Canvas
85 x 62 cm

41. *Portrait of Empress Elizabeth Alexeevna wife of Alexander I*
N. Tikhobrazov, 1810
Oil on canvas
65.5 x 54.3 cm

42. Armchair belonging to Alexander I
Tula,
late 18th - early 19th century
Polished steel, gilded bronze, velvet
95.5 x 72 x 56 cm

43. Foot Stool
Tula, early 19th century
Steel, velvet
20 x 25.5 x 33 cm

44. Salt-cellar of Alexander I from the Winter Palace
Moscow, early 19th century
Silver
17.5 x 9.5 x 9.5 cm

45. Razor of Alexander I
Moscow, 1818
Gold, silver, mother-of-pearl, steel
14.5 x 2.5 cm

46. Cameo with portraits of Alexander I and Elizabeth Alexeevna
Russia, early 19th century
Glass
4 x 4.6 cm

47. Snuff-box with a portrait of Alexander I
Veliky Ustiug, 1804-1809
Master, I Zhilin
Silver, niello
1.5 x 9 x 5.3 cm

48. Gospel from the field chapel of Alexander I
Russia, mid-18th century
Paper, gilded silver, silk, wood
19.8 x 16.5 cm

49. Icon belonging to Alexander I
Moscow, 1813
Gilded silver, enamel, wood, tempera
24.3 x 19.7 cm

Gift of the citizens of Pskov

50. Icon of the *Shuisky Smolensk Mother of God* with Oklad
Russia, late18th century
Wood, tempera, canvas, oklad of glass beads and embroidery
30 x 25 cm

51. Icon of *St.Nicholas* with Oklad
Russia, early 18th century
Wood, tempera, gold, silver, emeralds, glass, velvet
20.7 x 17.4 cm

52. Earrings with Portraits of Alexander I and Elizabeth Alexeevna
Russia, early 19th century
Gold, gouache, ivory
2.8 x 1.8 cm

53. Charger of Dowager Empress Maria Fedorovna, wife of Paul I, presented by the Merchants Society
Moscow, 1826
Gilded silver
55.8 cm in diam.

54. *Parade on Palace Square in St. Petersburg*
A.I. Ladurner and
E.D. Tiedemann, 1855
Oil on canvas
69.5 x 97.5 cm

55. Chiffre of Lady-in-Waiting to Maria Fedorovna, wife of Paul I
Russia, early 19th century
Gold
6 x 4.8 cm

56. *Portrait of Empress Maria Fedorovna*
Vetluzki 1828, from the original by George Dawe
Lithograph
54 x 42 cm

57. Prayer Gospel
Moscow, 1810
Gilded silver, velvet, enamel,
glass, paper
23.5 x 18 x 5 cm

60. *Portrait of Empress
Alexandra Fedorovna*
wife of Nicholas I
Franz Krueger, circa 1830
Oil on canvas
135 x 92 cm

63. Portfolio in red Morocco
leather with gold stitching,
for diplomatic papers
belonged to D.P.
Troschinsky
Western Europe,
late 18th century
41 x 33 cm

66. Cuff bracelet
Moscow, circa 1860
Gold, enamel, rubies, pearls
5.6 x 7.4 x 6.8 cm

58. Cameo with Portrait of
Nicholas I
Russia, 1828
Jasper
6.1 cm in diam.

61. Chalice
Moscow, 1787
Gilded silver
27.8 cm in height

64. Earrings
Russia, 1845
Gold, enamel
7.8 x 2.3 cm

67. Comb ornament
St. Petersburg,
early 19th century
Master I. Bergstrom
Horn, gold, agate, enamel,
diamonds
15.2 x 9.3 cm

59. Ring presented by Nicholas I
Russia, mid-19th century
Gold, silver, diamonds,
enamel
1.5 x 2 x 2 cm

62. Pair of Malachite Vases
Russia, mid-19th century
36 x 32 x 32 cm

65. Earrings
Russia, early 19th century
Rock crystal, gold
6.4 cm long

68. Signet ring presented by
Alexander I
Russia, early 19th century
Silver, agate, rose diamonds
2.5 x 3.2 x 2.7 cm

Checklist of Objects

Siberia and the Russian Merchants

69. Sled
    Russian North, 19th century
    Wood, iron, carving, painted
    decoration
    28.5 x 63 x 27 cm

73. "Coachman" bell
    Sculptor, E.A. Lanceret
    Russia, circa 1870
    Bronze, silver gilt
    11 x 6.5 cm

77. Wooden mold for prianiki
    (gingerbread) with carved
    design of a general
    Tver, circa 1830
    Wood, carving
    36 x 31 x 3.5 cm

81. Molded gingerbread in the
    form of a sterlet
    Tver, late 19th –
    early 20th century
    Preserved dough
    28 cm in diam.

70. Equestrian shaft-bow for a
    troika
    Volga region,
    late19th century
    Wood, iron, carving, painted
    decoration
    88 x 97.5 x 6 cm

74. Coach bell with inscription
    Russia, Valdai, 1812
    Bronze, iron, leather
    11.5 x 11.5 cm
    Inscription: *1812. This bell
    was cast in Valdai.
    To whom I love this I give.*

78. Molded gingerbread in the
    form of a general
    Tver, late 19th – early
    20th century
    Preserved dough
    17.5 x 17 cm

82. *Portrait of a Siberian
    Merchant's Wife*
    Unknown artist
    Russia, circa 1810
    Oil on canvas
    106 x 85 cm

71. Coachman's festive gauntlets
    Torzhok, 18th century
    Leather, red silk, gold
    embroidery
    34 cm in length

75. *The Water Carrier*, mujik
    breaking up ice
    Gardner Porcelain Factory,
    Verbilki, Moscow province
    late 19th century
    27.3 cm in height

79. Wooden mold for wedding
    prianiki (gingerbread)
    Volga region
    early 19th century
    Wood, carving
    41.5 x 32 x 5 cm

83. *Portrait of a St. Petersburg
    Merchant*
    Unknown artist
    Russia, circa 1800
    Oil on canvas
    101 x 88 cm

72. Coachman's hat
    Russia, 18th century
    Black velvet, silk
    60 x 28 cm

76. Festive Dress of a Woman of
    the North
    Kargopol region, late 18th –
    early 19th century
    Quilted sarafan, vest, blouse,
    scarf, headdress

80. Wooden mold for prianiki in
    the form of the emblem of
    the Russian Empire
    Russia, late 19th century
    Wood, carving
    22.5 x 21.5 x 4.5 cm

84. *Veliky Ustiug, Panoramic
    View of the City from the
    River*
    Vasily K. Berezin, 1795
    Oil on canvas
    351 x 71.5 cm

85. Inkwell
    Veliky Ustiug,
    late 17th – early 18th century
    Copper, colored enamel
    12.5 x 8 x 6.5 cm

86. Pendant earrings
    Northern Volga region,
    late 17th-early 18th century
    Copper, beads, glass
    4.5 x 8 cm

87. Blue (golubtsy) earrings
    Veliky Ustiug,
    late 17th – early 18th century
    Copper, white metal, colored
    enamel
    2.5 x 5 cm

88. Small round box
    Russia, 18th century
    Reed, silver, velvet
    2.7 x 6.3 x 5.2 cm

89. Small round box
    Russia, 18th century
    Reed, silver, Morocco leather
    3.5 x 5.5 x 4.2 cm

90. Small round box
    Russia, 18th century
    Reed, silver, velvet
    3 x 4.3 cm

91. Wedding chest
    Russia, early 18th century
    Wood, gilding, carving,
    painting
    57 x 45 x 35 cm

92. *Bridal Party before the
    wedding in Toropets*
    Artist unknown, late
    18th century
    Oil on canvas
    69 x 86.5 cm

93. Cover of a trunk with the
    image of Peter I
    Veliky Ustiug,
    early 18th century
    Wood, painting
    21 x 45 x 33.5 cm

94. Lacquered box with winter
    scene and troika
    Moscow region,
    Vishniakov factory,
    circa 1880
    Papier mache, metal,
    lacquer, painting
    5.5 x 15 x 9.5 cm

95. Tankard
    Archangel region,
    Northern Dvina,
    late 19th century
    Wood, carving, painting
    18 x 19 cm

96. Kovsh-Ladle
    Vologda region, 18th century
    Wood, carving, painting
    16 x 12 x 24 cm

97. Salt-cellar
    Vologda region, 18th century
    Wood, carving, painting
    14 x 24 x 10,5 cm

98. Candle box
    Vologda region, 18th century
    Wood, carving, painting
    8 x 37 x 10 cm

99. Festive serving dish (Kovsh)
    Archangel region,
    Northern Dvina,
    early 19th century
    Wood, carving, painting
    11 x 61,5 x 31,2 cm

100. Small serving dish (Kovsh)
     Vologda region
     19th century
     Wood, carving
     15 x 7.4 cm

Checklist of Objects

101. *Strolling on the Hills of Nijny Tagil*
Artist, I.P. Hudoyarov, 1840
Oil on metal
53 x 70 cm

102. Prialka (device for making linen thread) with the image of Nicholas I and Alexandra Fedorovna
Archangel region, Northern Dvina, late 19th century
Wood, carving, painting
89 x 18.5 x 53 cm

Traditional gift to a country bride

103. Architectural panel
Nijny Novgorod region, late 19th century
Pine, carving, tempera colors
32.5 x 260 x 7 cm

104. Architectural panel
Nijny Novgorod region, late 19th century
Pine, carving, tempera colors
29 x 214 x 7 cm

105. Architectural window frame
Volga region, late 19th century
Wood, carving
178 x 125 x 22 cm

106. Water flask for travel
Russia, 19th century
Wood, leather, carving, tempera colors
27 x 20.5 cm

107. Covered dish for travel
Archangel region, Northern Dvina
19th century
Wood, design in tempera colors
13 x 16 cm

108. Spoon for travel
Archangel region, Northern Dvina, early 19th century
Wood, carving, tempera colors
9.5 cm long

109. Salt-cellar for travel
Russian North, early 19th century
Birch, wicker
10 x 16 x 8.5 cm

110. Barrel for water
Siberia, 1892
Wood, metal, oil colors
56 x 50 x 52 cm

111. Svetez (device for lighting lamps)
Russia, late 17th – early 18th century
Wood, metal, carving
94 x 26.5 x 25.5 cm

112. Warehouse lock
Russia, late 17th – early 18th century
Wood, iron, carving
27.5 x 38 x 8 cm

113. Inkwell in the form of a merchant drinking tea
Russia, mid - 19th century
Bronze, gilding, malachite
19 x 23 x 15 cm

114. Statuette of a "Sbitenschik" (seller of a popular spiced honey drink)
Russia, mid - 19th century
Bronze, silver, gilding
19 x 9.5 x 12 cm

115. Shawl with lilacs
Nijny Novgorod province, peasant manufactory of N.A. Merlina, circa 1830
Hand woven wool
139 x 137 cm

116. *Healing Flowers and Herbs*
Manuscript book
Russia, late 18th – early 19th century
Manuscript, drawings
21.5 x 17.5 x 5.8 cm

117. Book mark
     Russia, late 18th century
     Glass beads
     10 x 11 x 3.5 cm

118. Carved ivory trunk
     Yakutia, 1799
     14.3 x 21.7 x 15 cm

119. Kvasnik (pitcher for Kvas,
     the traditional Russian
     fermented beverage)
     G'zhel, 1793
     Majolica, polychrome
     30 cm in height

120. Ethnographic variation of
     the map of the First
     Kamchatka
     Expedition (1725-1740) of
     V. Bering
     Unknown author,
     mid 18th century
     Paper, drawing, watercolors,
     India ink
     62 x 132 cm

121. Copy of the Ethnographic
     map
     46 x 88 cm

122. Festive girl's dress of the
     Evenky tribe of Northeastern
     Siberia
     Siberia, late 19th century
     Deer skin, leather, beads

123. Ritual ball of the Chukchi
     tribe of Siberia
     Siberia, late 19th century
     Leather, seal fur
     66 cm in diam.
     24 cm in ht.

124. Charka of Siberian Governor
     Chicherin
     Siberia, late 18th century
     Gilded silver, niello
     3 x 9 cm

125. Beaker of Siberian Governor
     Denis Chicherin
     Siberia, 1780
     Silver, niello
     10 x 7.3 x 7.3 cm

126. Snuff-box with Niello map
     of the cities of Siberia; on
     the interior is a Portrait of
     Governor D.I. Chicherin
     Siberia, 18th century
     Silver, niello, oil, canvas
     4.1 x 10.4 x 6.4 cm

127. Snuff-box with Niello map
     of the Aleutian Islands
     Siberia, mid-19th century
     Silver, niello
     2.6 x 8.5 x 8.5 cm

128. Ceremonial Bulava, symbol
     of the power of a Cossack
     Ataman
     Russia, 18th century
     Wood, silver, engraving,
     niello
     58 cm in length

129. General map of the Russian
     Empire from the Russian
     Atlas of 1792
     Engraving, watercolors
     74 x 159 cm

Checklist of Objects

Voyages to the New World

130. Mast of a river vessel in the
form of the sun
Volga region,
early 18th century
Wood, carving,
tempera colors
345 x 112 x 18 cm

131. Steering wheel of a ship
Russia, early 20th century
Wood, metal
128 cm in diam.

132. Sculpted icon of
St. Nicholas of Mozhaisk
Russia, 17th century
Wood, carving,
tempera colors
83 x 64 x 11 cm

133. Sculpted icon of
St. Paraskeva Pyatnitsa
Russia, 17th century
Wood, carving,
tempera colors
55 x 42 x 5,5 cm

134. Model of the brig *Mercury*
St. Petersburg, 19th century
Carved wood with
textile sails
166 x 63 x 134 cm

135. *Portrait of I.F. Kruzenstern*
Unknown artist, 1830
Oil on canvas
94 x 73 cm

136. Atlas of Kruzenstern's voyage
around the world
St. Petersburg, 1814
Engraving, leather, gold
stamping
64.5 x 49 x 5 cm

137. Russian atlas of 1792
St. Petersburg, 1792
Engraving, leather, gold
stamping
56 x 45 x 5 cm

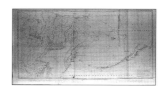

138. Map of the voyage of Billings
G.A. Sarychev 1795-1802
Engraving
74 x 134 cm

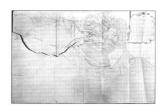

139. Map of Russian Exploration
of the Northern Pacific
Ocean
Draft of the Admiralty
College, 1780

140. Lt. L. Zagoskin's
descriptions of Russian
possessions in
America made during hiking
trips in 1842, 1843 and
1844
St. Petersburg
22.2 x 14.5 x 2.4 cm

141. *View of Petropavlovsk
Harbor on Kamchatka*
Unknown Artist
Russia, 1803 – 1806
Watercolor
27 x 30.7 cm

142. *Portrait of Admiral Yuri
Lisiansky* (1773-1837)
Engraving by A. Ukhtomsky,
1812 after the drawing by
G.J. Geusendam, 1812
15.3 x 11.6 cm

143. Map of Russian exploration
in the Northern Pacific
I. Truscott 1754
Engraving,
55 x 76 cm

144. Fragments of three nails
from Bering's ship
Russia, circa 1740
9 x 2, 10 x 2, 12 x 2 cm

*Taken from the site of the
winter stay of the First
Kamchatka Expedition*

145. Trunk covered with seal fur
Russia, Kholmogory,
early 18th century
28 x 42 x 25.5 cm

146. Pendant inkwell
Veliky Ustiug,
late 17th -
early 18th century
Copper, colored enamel
6.5 x 5 x 2.7 cm

147. Candlestick designed for use
on a ship
Russia or Europe,
late 19th century
Copper alloy, nickel
42.5 x 19 x 3 cm

148. *Deesis*, Triptych Icon
Russia, late 18th –
early 19th century
Copper, gilding, enamel
6 x 17 cm

149. Icon of St. *Nicholas the
Miracleworker*
Russia, late 19th century
Copper, enamel
30 x 26 cm

150. Telescope
London, late 18th century
Wood, brass, optical glass
60 x 6 cm

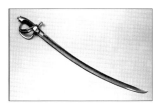

151. Sabre of a Naval officer
1855
Russia, Zlatoust,
Master T. Funslang
Steel, brass, leather, wood
96.5 x 80 x 3.5 cm

152. Ship's compass set in a
wooden box
Russia, mid- 19th century
Wood, brass, glass
10.5 x 18 x 19 cm

153. Measuring device
Western Europe,
early 17th century
18.2 x 2.1 x 1.4 cm

154. Scientific instrument with
sun-dial in a case
Russia, late 18th century
Brass, wood, engraving
14 x 12.5 x 5.5 cm

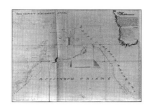

155. Map of Russian exploration
of the Northern Pacific
Ocean, 1787
Watercolors and India ink
120 x 160 cm

156. Map of the organization of
Russian trade in the
Northern Pacific
St. Petersburg, Geographical
Department of the Academy
of Science
Illuminated engraving
60 x 83. cm

157-158.
Cabin doors of a river ship
Volga region, 19th century
Wood, carving
tempera colors
149 x 52 x 3 cm,
150 x 50.5 x 3 cm

159. Medal awarded to
Lt. Ivan Kobelev, 1793
Copper
53.3 mm

160. Medal for a Pacific
expedition
Cast iron
82 mm

Checklist of Objects

The Russian American Company

161. *Portrait of G.I. Shelikhov*
V. Ivanov, after 1795
Etching
42 x 36 cm

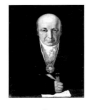

162. *Portrait of A.A. Baranov*
(1746-1819)
M.T. Tikhanov, circa 1810
Oil on canvas
69 x 54 cm

163. Medal presented to
*Kargopol Merchant
Baranov for his diligence
in directing and expanding
Russian trade in America*
Copper
44.9 mm

164. Medal with the inscription
Allies of Russia
Early 19th century
Silver
33.2 mm

165. Medal for the native peoples
of Northern Russia and the
indigenous peoples of
America, 1791
Copper
51.8 mm

166. *Portrait of Nicholas
Rezanov*
Unknown artist,
early 19th century
Oil on canvas
67 x 54 cm

167. Officer's formal pipe
(smoking) with amber
mouthpiece
Russia, early 19th century
Horn, amber, canvas,
beading, silk
75 x 6 cm

168. Tobacco box
Russia, early 19th century
Leather, beading, gilded
bronze
12.5 x 8.5 cm

169-171.
Parchment currency used by
the Russian- American
Company in North America
Russia, mid-19th century
10 kopecks, 60 x 51 mm
1 ruble, 66 x 47 mm
5 rubles, 70 x 50 mm
Leather parchment,
engraving

172. *View of New Archangel,
1851*
A.V. Prohorov
Lithograph
37.2 x 56

173. Abacus
Russia,
late 18th –
early 19th century
Ivory, metal
30 x 21 cm

174. Cotton scarf
Moscow, Titov factory
circa 1830
115 x 108 cm

175. Samovar-vase
Moscow,
Factory of D.A. Borisova
circa 1840
Copper, silver plate
43 x 34 x 41 cm

176. Rectangular Tray
Russia, Factory of K.R. Petza
circa 1840
Copper, silver plate
81 x 57 x 1.5 cM

177. *Residents of New Archangel*
G. Kittlitz, mid-19th century
Engraving
24 x 28 cm

178. *Koloshi* – natives of Russian
America in New Archangel
G. Kittlitz, mid-19th century
Engraving
24 x 28 cm

179. *Man of Kodiak Island*
N.I. Utkin 1802, from the atlas of Sarychev
Engraving
24 x 18.5 cm

180. *The Russian-American Company ship "Kutuzov" under the command of Captain Lt. Dokturov entering New Archangel Harbor on a moonlit night in the fall of 1821*
Lithograph, artist unknown
Early 19th century
40.7 x 50.8 cm

181. *People of North America* – four standing figures with attributes of fishing and hunting
Author unknown,
Mid-18th century
Engraving
31.5 x 20 cm

182. *Portrait of Grand Duke Michael Pavlovich*
Shareholder of the Russian-American Company
Engraving by F.I. Jordan 1838, from the original by I.K. Kanevsky 1837
36 x 29 cm

183. *Portrait of Grand Duke Konstantin Pavlovich*
Shareholder of the Russian-American Company
Watercolor by J.I. Lukashevich
34.5 x 29 cm

184. List of shareholders of the Russian-American Company
St. Petersburg,
December 15, 1825
36 x 22 cm

185. List of commodities received in Okhotsk by the Russian-American Company, brought from the Aleutian Islands (indicating their quality and cost)
1st half of the 19th century
31.5 x 91.5 cm

186. Declaration of the sale of shares of the Russian-American Company to a merchant in Veliky Ustiug, Fedor Yegorovich Shergin
Early 19th century
26 x 19 cm

187. Mask of the Water Spirit
Native tribe of Kamchatka
Early 20th century
Deer skin, hair
35 cm in height

188. *Portrait of Princess A.A. Volkonsky*
Circa 1760
Artist unknown
Oil on canvas
59.3 x 48.8 cm

189. *Portrait of a Merchant's Wife with Fur Muff*
Artist unknown
late 18th –
early 19th century
Oil on canvas
86 x 71 cm

Checklist of Objects

St. Innokenty, Enlightener of the Aleuts

190. *Portrait of Metropolitan Innokenty*
Engraving, late 19th century
42.3 x 29.3

191. *Two Panoramic Views of the Cities of Irkutsk and Yakutia, 1770*
Etching by A.G. Rudakov
44 x 54.5 cm

192. Vestment of an Orthodox Deacon (Stichar)
Russia, early 19th century
Velvet, silk, gold thread
142 cm in height

193. Illuminated Manuscript of the *Apocalypse*
includes 72 miniatures (tempera and gold)
Cover: wood, leather, copper
37 x 23 x 6 cm

194. Mitre of a Bishop
Russia, early 19th century with decorations from the 17th, 18th centuries
Gold, silver, pearls, diamonds, sapphires, rubies, emeralds, enamel, velvet, silk
23.2 cm in height

195. Wedding Crowns
St. Petersburg,
Early 19th century
Gilded silver, enamel, glass, velvet
23.5 x 27.0 x 27 cm

Crowns are held over the heads of the bride and groom during the Russian wedding service.

196. Altar Cross
Moscow, 1835
Gilded silver, turquoise, glass
35.5 x 22.2 cm

197. Diskos (dish for the Eucharist)
Moscow, 1783,
Master F. Stydentsev
Gilded silver
12.5 x 28.8 x 28.8 cm

198. Zvyesditsa (cover for Eucharist)
Moscow, 1768
Gilded silver, glass, enamel
10.3 cm in height

199. Vessel for the reserved Eucharist
Russia, early 19th century
Gilded silver
40.2 cm in ht.

200. Censer
St. Petersburg, 1775
Gilded silver
22.5 cm high

201. Vestments of an Orthodox Priest
Podriznik, epitrachilion, sash, nabedrenik, phelon, porychi, pendant cross with chain, panagia with chain
Russia, late 19th century
Deer skin and embroidery

202-203.
Pair of Candle Stands
Russia, 1915
Wood, tempera colors, copper
125 x 35, 127 x 35 cm

204. Icon of *The Nativity*
Russian North, 16th century
Wood, tempera
91.5 x 61 cm

205. Icon of *The Presentation in the Temple*
Vologda, early 16th century
Wood, tempera
82 x 61.5 cm

209. *Man from the Island of Unalaska*
N. Utkin, 1802,
from the atlas of Sarychev
Etching
24 x 18.5 cm

213. *Portrait of Metropolitan Philaret (Drozdov) of Moscow* (1782-1867)
Artist unknown,
Mid-19th century
Oil on canvas
80.2 x 62 cm

217. Extract of a letter of the
Nushagak missionary,
Hieromonk Feofil
of January 20, 1859
to Archbishop Innokenty
25.5 x 21.5 cm

206. Icon of *St. Basil the Great*
Tver School,
late 16th century
Wood, tempera
94 x 34 cm

210. *Man and Woman from the Island of Unalaska in Native Dress*
Etching, early 19th century,
artist unknown
26.5 x 21.5 cm

214. Message signed by
Metropolitan Philaret,
Metropolitan of Moscow
35.5 x 22 cm

218. Letter of Metropolitan
Innokenty of Moscow to
Bishop Leonid of Dmitrov of
March 7, 1868
with signature
27 x 21 cm

207. Icon of *The Three Hierarchs, Sts. Basil the Great, Gregory the Theologian and John Chrysostom*
Kholmogory, 16th century
Wood, tempera
119 x 88.5 cm

211. *Woman from the Island of Unalaska*
N. Utkin, 1802,
from the atlas of Sarychev
Etching
24.5 x 19 cm

215. *View of the Trinity St. Sergius Monastery*
Peter C. Stepanov, 1866
Oil on canvas
63 x 93.5 cm

219. Photograph of Metropolitan
Innokenty with his son and
grandson.
Photograph by F. Osipov,
Trinity-St. Sergius Lavra,
1860's
10.5 x 6.8 cm

208. *Woman from Kodiak Island*
N. Utkin, 1802
Etching
24.5 x 18.5 cm

212. Walrus Tusk with engraved
figures of native people,
igloos and reindeer
19th century
56 cm in length

216. *Portrait of Ioann, Bishop of the Aleutian Islands*
L. Seryakov
Color lithograph from a
photograph of 1871
14.5 x 12.2 cm

220. *Portrait of Nicholas I*
A. Poliakov, 1829
Oil on canvas
73 x 62 cm

Checklist of Objects

Moscow and the Coronation of Alexander II

221. Equestrian harness and head gear made for the Coronation of Alexander II
St. Petersburg,
Valter and Cox, 1857
Bronze, silver, brass, leather, velvet, gold thread, horse hair, gilding, neeldework
Headgear, bridle, and blind ers 140cm in length
Saddle with fastening belts, 209 cm in length, 13 cm in width

222. *Portrait of Tsarevich Alexander Nicholaevich*
Vologda, 1838,
Master S. Skripitsin
Silver, niello, wood, copper
29.7 x 27.7 cm

223. *Portrait of Alexander II on a Horse*
N.E. Sverchkov, 1871
Oil on canvas
74 x 98 cm

224. Uniform of a Minister of the Imperial Court of the First Rank
Russia, late 19th – early 20th century
Broadcloth, gold thread, spangles, silk
90 cm in length

225. Formal Trousers of the Uniform
Russia, late 19th – early 20th century
White broadcloth, decorative galloon trim
108 cm in length

226. Three-cornered Hat of a Courtier
Russia, late 19th – early 20th century
Felt, gold thread, ostrich feathers
44 x 9 cm

227. *Winter Races at the Petrovsky Palace on the Outskirts of Moscow*
A.A. Golitsyn, 1848
Oil on canvas
50 x 68 cm

228. *View of the Moscow Kremlin from the Sofia Embankment*
Peter P. Vereschagin, 1868
Oil on canvas
66 x 103 cm

229. *Triumphant Procession on Ivanov Square of the Moscow Kremlin after the Coronation of Alexander II in the Uspensky Cathedral,* 1856
Gustav Schwartz
Oil on canvas
71 x 109 cm

230. Declaration of the Coronation of Alexander II and Maria Alexandrovna in Moscow on August 26, 1856
St. Petersburg,
Lithograph by A. Petersen, 1856
Color lithograph
28 x 21.5 cm

231. Menu for the Banquet in the Grand Kremlin Palace in honor of the Coronation of Alexander III and Maria Fedorovna,
Moscow, May 15, 1883
V.M. Vasnetsov
Color Lithograph
80 x 27 cm

232. Portrait Badge with Alexander II and Alexander III *presented to Prince A.M. Gorchakov in 1881*
Russia, 1881
Leopold Selftigen, Court Jeweler
Gold, silver, tempera, paste
8.4 x 5 cm

233. Diptych with the Legacy of
Alexander II to all the
Guards
St. Petersburg, 1867,
Master, Sokolov
Silver, enamel
17.5 x 23.3 cm

234. Icon of the *Smolensk
Mother of God* belonging
to Alexander II
Moscow, 1854,
Firm of Sazikov
Wood, tempera, silver,
enamel, sapphires, rubies
25 x 20 cm

235. Signet ring given by
Alexander II with his
portrait
Russia, 1855-1881
Gold, silver, rock crystal,
ivory, gouache
2.8 x 2.8 x 2.8 cm

236. *Portrait of
Prince A.M. Gorchakov*
N. Bogatsky, 1876
Oil on canvas
76.7 x 60.5 cm

237. Gramota with Seal awarded
by Alexander II to General-
Adjutant, Vice-Admiral E.V.
Putiatin granting the Title of
Count. Given for the signing
of an agreement with Japan
St. Petersburg,
November 20, 1869
Gold, velvet, parchment,
silk, gold thread,
watercolors and wax
61.6 x 48.5 cm,
diameter of seal 28 cm

238. *Portrait of E.V. Putiatin*
Pasheny, lithograph, 1857-
1863
50 x 36.5 cm

239. Tankard of E.V. Putiatin
St. Petersburg, 1856
Master, Karl Simonson
Silver
30.8 cm in ht.

240. *Portrait of N.I. Guchkov*
(1860-1935) President of
the Russian-American
Chamber of Commerce in
Moscow
Photo tint
early 20th century
21 x 14.7 cm

241. Pair of Standing
Candelabras
Russia, late 19th century
Gilded bronze
90.5 x 43 x 19 cm

242. *Moscow Service* coffee set
with images of architectural
monuments of Moscow
Moscow,
Firm of P. Ovchinnikov
1884
8 cups and saucers with tray
Gilded silver, niello
Tray: 57 x 36.8 cm;
cups:5.7 x 4.3 cm;
saucers:10,7 cm in diam.

243. Easter Egg
Moscow, 1896-1908
Imperial Stroganov School
Silver, enamel, amondine
6.5 x 5.2 x 5.2 cm

244. Coffee and Tea Service
in Russian style.
Moscow, 1908-1917,
Firm of O. Kurliukov
10 pieces: teapot, coffee
pot, jam dish, sugar bowl,
biscuit dish, spoon for
lemon, sugar scoop, sugar
tongs, teaspoon, coffee spoon
Silver, enamel,
mother-of-pearl

245. *Cockerel* Wine Set
Moscow, 1875-1885,
Firm of I. Khlebnikov
7 pieces: carafe, tray,
5 charkas
Silver, enamel
Tray: 48.9 x 39.4 cm;
carafe: 38.5 x 31 x 18cm,
charkas (5): 6,5 x 9,7 x 6 cm

246. Box of Grand Duke Alexis
Alexandrovich with images
of cruisers:
"Pamyat Azova", "Admiral
Nahimov", "Vladimir
Monomach" "Admiral
Kornilov",
rowboats: "Manchuria",
"Koraietz", "Sivych", "Bobr"
St. Petersburg, 1880-90,
Firm of Faberge,
Workmaster Y. Rappoport
Silver
8.4 x 20.4 x 14 cm

247. *Portrait of Grand Duke
Alexis Alexandrovich*
A.G. Pirogova, circa 1910
Color photoprint
49 x 27.9 cm

248. Table Clock
St. Petersburg, 1903-1908
Firm of Faberge
Workmaster, Wigstrom
Gold, silver, enamel, ivory,
metal
16.1 x 10.9 cm

249. Cigarette Case of Grand
Duke Konstantin
Konstantinovich
St. Petersburg,
late 19th century
Firm of Faberge,
Workmaster, Edward
Schramm
Gold, sapphire
1.9 x 8.7 x 6.1 cm

250. Cigarette Case of Grand
Duke Konstantin
Konstantinovich
St. Petersburg, 1896-1908
Firm of Grachev Brothers
Gold, Silver
2.1 x 10.4 x 8.0 cm

251. Court Dress of Grand
Duchess Maria Fedorovna
wife of the
future Alexander III
Russia, 1866
Lace, satin, velvet, swan fur,
gold and silver thread
Train is 3 m long,
150 cm ht.

252. Ashtray in the form of a
dolphin
Moscow, 1908-1917,
Firm of Faberge
Silver
8.5 x 10.2 x 12.6 cm

253. Brooch
Moscow, late 19th century
Master I. Chichelev
Gold, enamel, rubies,
sapphires, diamonds, pearl
6 x 5.5 cm

254. Bouillon Urn
Moscow, 1808-1867
Firm of Sazikov,
Workmaster I. Zaitsev
Silver
45 cm in ht.

255. Desk Set
5 pieces: inkwell, saucer,
pen, 2 candlesticks
Moscow, 1883,
Firm of P. Ovchinnikov
Gilded silver, enamel
Inkwell: 16 x 11.5 x 11.5 cm;
saucer, 20.7 cm in diam.;
pen: 16.3 cm long;
Candlesticks: 13.9 x 8 x 8 cm

256. Cigarette Case, *Frost*
Moscow, 1906,
Firm of Faberge
Silver, sapphire, diamonds,
metal
4.1 x 18.9 x 13 cm

257. Biscuit Dish
Moscow, 1880,
Firm of I.Khlebnikov
Silver
9.5 x 28.4 x 19.5 cm

258. Tray with a winter scene,
Sliding Hills on the
Neglinka River in the
Moscow Kremlin during
Maslenitsa
Russia, early 19th century
Iron, painting, lacquer
5.5 x 77.5 x 56.3 cm

259. Fabric sample of the
Olovyanishnikov
Association, member of the
Russian-American Chamber
of Commerce
Russia, early 20th century
Brocade fabric with gold
thread
86 x 56.5 cm

260. Fabric sample of the
Olovyanishnikov Association
Russia, early 20th century
Brocade fabric with gold
thread
45 x 79 cm

261. Pieces from the Dessert
Service of Grand Duke
Konstantin Nikolaevich
St. Petersburg,
Imperial Porcelain Factory,
1848
Artist, F.G. Solntsev
Porcelain, gilding, painting,
quilloche
Wine cooler, 20.5 cm
in height
Covered cup with saucer,
11.2 in height,
17.3 in diameter
Dessert plate,
22.5 cm in diameter

262. Photograph of Grand Duke
Konstantin Nicholaevich
F. Orlov, Yalta, circa 1880
21.5 x 13.9 cm

263. Sculpture, *Leo Tolstoy at*
Work
Ilya Y. Ginzberg, 1891
Bronze
29.5 x 19.5 x 21.5 cM

264. Letter of Leo Tolstoy in
English to the North
American newspaper
Philadelphia on his
attitude toward the Russo-
Japanese War, in English.
Yasnaya Polyana, signature
of Tolstoy
1904-1905,
14.7 x 8.9 cm

265. Letter of Thomas Jefferson
to Jean Batiste Say, a French
economist, in connection
with his recent work.
Monticello, May 14, 1817,
signature of Jefferson
42.5 x 26 cm

266. Folder with an address to
V.A. Dolgorukoff, Governor
General of Moscow from the
American residents of
Moscow on the occasion of
the 25th anniversary of his
governor ship
August 31, 1890
Leather, wood, copper,
etching, watercolors
48 x 37.5 cm

Checklist of Objects

From the State Archives of the Russian Federation

267. *Siberia and its Villages*,
brochure by George Kennan
St. Petersburg, 1906

268. Statement of the peasants of
Alexandrovka, Tambov
Province, expressing their
gratitude to the American
people for sending bread
during the famine year of
1892.

269. *America in Petersburg*,
brochure on friendly
relations between Russia
and America
St. Petersburg, 1866

270. Notes of Grand Duke
Konstantin Nicholaevich to
A.M. Gorchakov on the
activities of the Russian-
American Company and the
necessity of changing its
statutes.
1857

271. Address of citizens of the
USA to Alexander II
expressing gratitude for
sympathy and support during
the War Between the States.
1865
70 x 50 cm

From the National Archives of the United States

272. Letter of Alexander II to President Lincoln, dated July 6, 1862. Contained in the diplomatic volume *Communications from Russia*

273. Draft of a letter from President Lincoln to Alexander II dated September 6, 1862. Two loose pages

From the State of Alaska, Department of History and Archaeology

274. Castle Hill, Sitka Lithograph, 1827

275. Castle Hill, Sitka Lithograph, 1868

276. Castle Hill, Sitka Photograph, circa 1890

277. The Castle Burning Photograph, 1894

Artifacts found on the site of Castle Hill, Sitka, 1997-1998

278. Lead Seal with the stamp of the Russian-American Company

279. Buttons

280. Quill tips

281. Violin tuners

282. 16 lb. Cannonball

283. Turkish pipe

284. Ivory chesspiece

285. Triptych panel (from an icon)

286. Chandelier crystals

287. Pendant crosses

288. Russian coin

289. Polished agate jewelry

290. Russian uniform button

291. Carved ivory bear

292. Carved ivory birds

293. Cross

294. "RAC" lead seals

295. Crystal decanter stopper, circa 1800

296. Chinese Export porcelain fragments

297. Copper salt spoon

From the collection of John C. Middleton, Pacific Grove, California

298. Flag of the Russian-American Company St. Petersburg, 1992 Vladimir Naval Flag Factory Wool, linen, linen rope 34 x 60 inches

Designed in 1806, the flag was approved by Alexander I for the exclusive use of the Russian-American Company. It is based on the Russian merchant flag with the addition of the Imperial eagle and a banner on which is written, Russian-American Company. The flag was flown on all company ships and at colonial sites such as Fort Ross in California and New Archangel (Sitka) in Alaska, indicating the relationship of the Company with the Russian government.

Biographical Index

Alexander I (1777-1825)

A grandson of Catherine the Great, and eldest son of Paul I, he became Emperor of Russia in 1801. When he ascended the throne he declared that he would reign in compliance with the laws and after the heart of Catherine the Great. He abolished many acts of Paul I and actively began to work out liberal reforms. His foreign policy was rather flexible, but eventually Russia was involved in a war with France. In June 1812 Napoleon's army of 600,000 invaded Russia without any declaration of war. A wave of unprecedented patriotic enthusiasm swept over the country. Both army and civilians participated in the war. Napoleon was particularly shocked to see Muscovites abandoning the city, leaving their homes and belongings, not wanting to see him. By Christmas, Russia was already celebrating victory. Napoleon was able to withdraw from Russia but his army had shrunk to 15,000. Since that time, Alexander I has been called Alexander the Blessed. Heralded as a savior by the Russian people, he became the leader of entire sections of Europe, though this honor became too much for him. He began to turn increasingly towards religion and his desire to live a private and secluded life became stronger. In 1825 he joined his wife in Taganrog where she was undergoing medical treatment. Soon after that, he contracted an illness and died.

Alexander II (1818-1881)

He became Emperor of Russia in 1855. He was a person of good disposition who was the product of a fine upbringing. He ascended to the throne at the age of 36 and at that time possessed sufficient experience in the affairs of state. While in power Alexander II was responsible for many important social reforms, the most renowned being the abolition of serfdom and the liberation of the serfs. He also implemented military, legal, censorship and educational reforms. Liberalization of national rules and regulations gave rise to a revolutionary movement. During his reign there were eight attempts on the Emperor's life. On March 1, 1881 he was mortally wounded during a terrorist attack in St. Petersburg.

Alexandra Fedorovna (1798-1860)

Born Frederica Louise Charlotte Wilhemine, the daughter of Frederic-Wilhelm III, the King of Prussia, she married Nicholas I in 1817.

Alexis Alexandrovich (1850-1908)

Grand Duke and the fourth son of Alexander II, his father prepared him for naval service from his birth. He became General-Admiral (1881-1905), the head of the Russian Navy and the Naval Department, succeeding Grand Duke Konstantin Nikolaevich in that position. During his service in the Navy Department many battleships and cruisers were built. It was rumored however, that he was not interested in anything but ships and women. Between 1871 and 1873 he took a voyage to the United States and was a great success with the American ladies.

Baranov, Alexander Andreevich (1746-1819)

Chief manager of the Shelikhov and RAC settlements in North America, 1790-1818. Born in Kargopol, northern Russia, in 1746, he engaged in trade there and then in Moscow and St. Petersburg, until 1780, when he set out for Siberia. Settling in Irkutsk, he established a glass factory and a distillery, and engaged in contracting and tax-farming. Some of his economic observations and experiments, conveyed to the Free Economic Society, led to his election to membership in that body in 1787.

G.I. Shelikhov proposed that Baranov become the manager of his North American enterprises; Baranov felt that had to accept. On 15 August 1790 Baranov and Shelikhov signed a contract in Okhotsk.

On 19 August, Baranov sailed from Okhotsk on the galiot *Tri Sviatitelia* for Kad'iak. On 28 September Baranov was forced by shortage of water to put in at Koshigin Bay, Unalaska. On the 30th they were ready to sail when a storm came up and during the night the vessel was wrecked. Left destitute, Baranov, the crew and the passengers had to take refuge at the settlement on Unalaska. During the winter he had three baidarkas built, and a census taken of the local population. In the spring of 1791, sending two baidarkas to seek new hunting areas, he set out to Kad'iak in the third. After a difficult voyage he and his party arrived on 27 June at Three Saints Bay, then the company center.

After examining various localities, in 1792 Baranov moved his headquarters to the site of present-day Kodiak. From there he began establishing other settlements and developing the sea otter trade, sending parties of Aleuts to Kenai Bay and along the Aliaska Peninsula. In June, returning from a trip to Chugash Bay, he and his men camped near Montague Island, and there fought off a night attack by the Yakut Kolosh (Tlingit) and Ugaliagmiuts from Cape St. Elias.

Biographical Index

In 1793, Baranov established a settlement on Chugach Bay, Voskresenkaia gavan' (harbor), or Ressurection Bay, (now Seward). There James Shields, a British shipbuilder in company service, began construction of the 3-masted Phoenix, the first ship built by the Russians in America. In 1794, Baranov sent Purtov and Kulikalov with an expedition to reconnoiter Yakutat Bay, while he went again to Chugach Bay with a fleet of 500 baidarkas. The British explorer, Captain George Vancouver, in the vicinity, tried unsuccessfully to meet the by now well-known Russian, but Baranov failed to keep three appointments, perhaps preferring to avoid committing himself regarding company plans. Returning to Kad'iak, Baranov was there on 24 September when the transport *Tri Sviatitelia* arrived from Okhotsk, bearing Archimandrite Ioasaf and a retinue of ten clerics, to found a spiritual mission in the New World, and on 24 October when another, the *Sv. Ekaterina*, arrived bearing 130 promyshlenniks and 30 settlers and their families. Both groups had been sent with government approval in response to urging by Shelikhov. The missionaries soon claimed thousands of converts among the local population. Though these conversions were at first superficial, they indicated a willingness to accept change, and were the basis of other, more lasting work by Orthodox clergy. Relations between Baranov and the missionaries, based on different motives, were often acrimonious.

In 1799, Baranov founded the fort of Novarkhangel'sk (Sitka), returning to Kad'iak on 20 April the following year. In 1802, the local Kolosh (Tlingit) burned Novarkhangel'sk and slew most of the inhabitants. In 1804, Baranov went from Kad'iak to Sitka with whatever company vessels were at hand, and a fleet of Aleut baidarkas and prepared to retake the site. Timely arrival of the round-the-world vessel Neva, under Lieutenant Lisianskii, helped ensure victory. Baranov built a new fort on the site of present-day Sitka, and transferred the center of Russian settlements from Kad'iak to Novoarkhangel'sk.

From his new capital, Baranov sent trading and exploring expeditions along the west coast to California. In 1804, on a share agreement, he sent the first of a number of fur trading parties from Kad'iak to the California coast on the Boston ship O'Cain (Capt. Joseph O'Cain). In 1812 his assistant I.A. Kuskov, founded the settlement of Ross, 50 miles north of the Spanish port of San Francisco.

Although he did remarkable work during his 28 years in North America, Bararnov's efforts were limited by the meager support provided by the RAC and the Russian government, and bad luck. An agreement in 1809 with John Jacob Astor's Pacific Fur Company, which might have had the double advantage of guaranteeing supplies and reducing the operations of New England fur traders on coasts claimed by Russia, fell through because of shipwreck and the war of 1812.

Baranov's evident physical and mental deterioration led on 1 January 1818 to his replacement by L.A. Hagemeister. In the fall of 1818, Baranov left Russian America on the ship *Kutuzov*, commanded by Hagemeister, bound for St. Petersburg, where he was to render the company an accounting for his 28-year stewardship. On 16 April 1819 he died on the homeward voyage. His body was committed to the waters of Sunda Strait.

Baranov's name is borne in Alaska by Baranov (earlier Sitkha) Island renamed in 1805 by Captain. F. Lisianskii; by the Baranof Archipelago, Baranof Lake and the Baranof River.

From Richard A. Pierce, *Russian America: A Biographical Dictionary*, reprinted with the gracious permission of The Limestone Press)

Bezborodko, Alexander Andreevich (1747-1799)

Count, diplomat, and prominent statesman during the reign of Catherine II, he possessed remarkable talents and a phenomenal memory. He could express himself in a laconic, precise and impressive style. It was he who wrote most of the acts signed by the Empress. He was an influential adviser to the Empress both in domestic and foreign affairs and the author of the most important instructions for Russian diplomats all over the world. He also was responsible for formulating the concept of armed neutrality at the time of the War for Independence in America. He was exceedingly devoted to his country and loved it a great deal. His favorite expression was: "Not a single cannon in Europe would dare to fire without our permission."

Golitsyn, Dmitry Mikhailovich (1721-1793)

Prince and diplomat, he played an important role in establishing trade relations between Russia and foreign countries. He was also a patron of scholars and artists, and had a magnificent collection of art, sculpture and bronzes. He contributed generously to various charities and made a provision in his will that after his death, all the serfs who had served him should be set free.

Goncharov, Ivan Alexandrovich (1812-1891)

Russian writer and author of a renowned set of sea voyage essays, he served as secretary aboard the ship Pallada that was involved in the Putiatin mission.

Gorchakov, Alexander Mikhailovich (1798-1883)

Prince and Minister of Foreign Affairs (1856-1882), he was a friend of A.S. Pushkin from their school days at the

Lyceum. Pushkin referred to the Prince with these lines: "a student of fashion, a friend of high society, a brilliant observer of customs." Prince Gorchakov's political views and ideas were shaped during the reign of Nicholas I, when it was expected that Russia would look after various European dynasties often to the detriment of her own interests. He stood for peace in the Balkans but, going against his principles, he was brought into a war there. His plan to be only partially involved in the war with the use of half-measures did not materialize. The war between Russia and Turkey turned out to be laborious and comparatively fruitless. During his rule Alexander II often relied on Gorchakov in matters of state. Gorchakov continually took a stand for a peaceful settlement of the issue of the Russian colonies in America. In 1871 he succeeded in reviewing the provisions of the Peace Treaty signed by Russia after her defeat in the Crimean war (1853-1856) which prevented her from having seaports and maintaining a navy in the Black Sea.

Guchkov, Nicholas Ivanovich (1860-1935)

Mayor of Moscow (1905-1913), Chairman of the Russian Duma (Parliament), and Chairman of the Military Industrial Committee, Guchkov descended from a family of former serfs. He graduated from the Law School of Moscow University. Later he had a tea trade business and served on the boards of Moscow and Petersburg Commercial Banks. Under his leadership the Moscow City economy became the most efficient in Russia. He was a founder of the Constitutional Democratic Party and did much charity work with Grand Duchess Elizabeth Feodorovna. He founded and became chairman of the Russian American Chamber of Commerce in 1913 in Moscow. All major American commerce centers sent him invitations to visit them. Guchkov emigrated from Russia in 1920 and lived abroad.

Dashkova, Catherine Romanovna, (Vorontsova) (1744-1810)

Princess and director of the Petersburg Academy of Science (1783-1796), she was an unusually gifted child with an outstanding personality. By the age of 15 she had read the complete works of Voltaire and Helvetian. Her sister was a favorite with Emperor Peter III. Princess Dashkova was involved in the palace coup. As a result of the coup Peter III was assassinated and his wife Catherine II ascended the throne. A few years later the relationship between Catherine II and Princess Dashkova became strained and the Princess was compelled to leave Russia. She traveled extensively in Europe; she met and corresponded with Voltaire, Montesquieu, and Benjamin Franklin. At Mr. Franklin's recommendation she was elected a member of the American Philosophy Society, while Mr. Franklin was elected a member of the Russian Academy of Science in 1789. The Empress offered Princess Dashkova the position of President of the Academy of Sciences. She accepted and proved herself to be a very energetic president and was accomplished at looking after the affairs of the Academy. When Paul I came to power Princess Dashkova was dismissed from her many positions and banished to the countryside. After Paul I died she was brought out of disgrace and devoted the rest of her life to literature. She had an exceedingly rich collection of mineral stones which she left to Moscow University.

Catherine II (1729-1796)

Born German Princess Sophia Frederica Augusta, she became Empress of Russia in 1762. Empress Elizabeth for a long time had been unable to select a bride for her nephew Peter (who would be Peter III) until she laid her eyes on the girl recommended by Frederick, King of Prussia. Peter III was not well liked by his people and in 1762 with the strong support of the guards Catherine staged a palace coup and as a result of the coup was put on the Russian throne. Thus began the reign of the famous Catherine the Great in a time often called the Golden Age. Empress Catherine enjoyed the reputation of a cultured and humane ruler and she also distinguished herself with an ability to choose people with proper capabilities for influential government positions. Under her leadership estates and cities were granted self-government. Russia conquered the Crimea and the northern shores of the Black Sea. The Empress loved literature and during her reign all levels of society experienced a cultural revival.

Elizabeth Alexeevna (1779-1826)

Born a German Princess Louise Marie Augusta, she was chosen by Catherine II herself as a bride for Alexander I. They were married in 1793. She was an unusually modest and extremely beautiful woman who pursued happiness in a quiet family life. Elizabeth gave birth to two girls but they died at an early age. She read extensively and could sing beautifully. In 1812 she absolutely refused to participate in all social events and devoted herself to charity. The Dowager Empress Maria Feodorovna, widow of Paul I, then assumed the center position at court. Near the end of her life, Empress Elizabeth's health was failing and doctors recommended that she go abroad, but she chose to continue with her life in Russia. Soon after the death of Alexander I, she also passed away.

Innokenty (Ivan Evseevich Popov-Veniaminov) (1797-1879)

Bishop of the Russian Orthodox church in Alaska and Metropolitan of Moscow, he was born Ioann Popov in Anginskoe (or Anga), Siberia, the son of Eusebius Popov, a church warden (or sacristan), and Thekla (maiden name unknown). His family was very poor. At the age of nine he began studies in the theological seminary at nearby Irkutsk. When he was seventeen years old, the principal of the seminary changed his last name to Veniaminov in honor of the late Bishop Benjamin, who had assumed the Russian form of his name at his ordination as bishop and whom the gifted student had spent much time visiting. When he was nineteen, seminarian Veniaminov married a local priest's daughter named Catherine Sharin; the couple had seven children. In 1821 he was ordained a priest and assigned as second priest in a parish in Irkutsk. Although happy with his life in the parish there, in 1823 he responded to his bishop's request for volunteers as missionaries to Alaska. He wrote later that after hearing about the Aleuts living there from an old adventurer, "I began to burn with desire to go to such a people!" He and his family left for Alaska in May 1823.

In 1824 Veniaminov began his pastoral work on Unalaska, one of the Aleutian Islands; he worked among the Aleut natives, the Russian fur traders in the area, and the "creoles" resulting from intermarriages between the two groups. Skilled in the building trades, he taught the Aleuts carpentry, masonry and metalworking, and together they built the Church of the Ascension in Harbor Village on Unalaska. Eager to learn all he could about the Aleuts and their culture, Veniaminov became fluent in their language, developed an alphabet for it, and wrote a dictionary, a grammar, and a primer that helped to promote literacy among children and adults. He wrote the first book published in the Unangan (Fox) Aleut dialect, *An Indication of the Pathway into the Kingdom of Heaven* (1833; English translation, 1976), and also translated the Gospel of Matthew, portions of the Gospel of Luke, and various prayers and liturgical texts into the language. In addition, he wrote a pioneering three-volume ethnographic work on the Aleuts and their land, *Notes on the Islands of the Unalaska District* (1839, 1840; English translation, 1984). (See page 35) He also established Alaska's first meteorological station. During his ten years of service on Unalaska he ministered throughout the Aleutian chain and supervised the

construction of a school, an orphanage, and numerous chapels on neighboring islands. In 1834 Veniaminov was transferred to New Archangel (now Sitka, Alaska), the administrative center of Russian America, where he immediately began working with area Tlingits. Once again he learned the native language and customs, translated sacred texts, and emphasized education. After a smallpox epidemic broke out early in 1836, he gradually was able to persuade the Tlingits to be vaccinated against the disease. This halted the outbreak of smallpox and greatly helped in the Tlingits' acceptance of the gospel. In 1838 and 1839 Veniaminov traveled to Saint Petersburg to arrange for the publication of his books, both in Russian and Aleut, and to ask that the church hierarchy create a separate diocese for Alaska (instead of being part of the Diocese of Irkutsk), which would train its own native clergy. In 1840, while in Russia, he received news of his wife's death in Irkutsk. He was then urged by the Synod of Bishops of the Russian church to accept monastic tonsuring and consecration as bishop of the new diocese whose establishment he was supporting. On 15 December 1840, in Saint Petersburg, he was consecrated Bishop Innokenty of Kamchatka and the Kurilian and Aleutian Islands.

From his administrative headquarters in Sitka, Veniaminov furthered the missionary work throughout the islands and into the interior of Alaska, setting an outstanding example for his priests by continuing to make long pastoral journeys by kayak and dogsled even in the harsh winter months. One trip, in 1842-1843, covered roughly 12,500 miles throughout his entire diocese. Also as bishop, he oversaw construction of the Mission House in Sitka, the oldest standing building in Alaska; its Annunciation Chapel is the oldest Orthodox church in continuous use in the Western Hemisphere. The first Orthodox seminary in the New World was established at the Mission House in 1845, and three years later the first Orthodox cathedral, Saint Michael the Archangel, was consecrated in Sitka; of the nearly fifty

Alaskan clergy who were present, most were natives or creoles. In 1852, now archbishop, Innokenty was given charge of the Yakutsk diocese in Siberia. Dividing his time between Alaska and eastern Asia, he undertook similar missionary and linguistic endeavors in Yakutsk. Documenting the success of the Archbishop's work in Alaska, a government report compiled in 1860 mentioned some 12,000 native Alaskan Christians, forty-four parish churches or chapels, seventeen schools, and several orphanages. In 1867, with the sale of Alaska to the United States, the archbishop urged the Holy Synod of the Russian church to transfer the church headquarters from Alaska to San Francisco and to promote English as the main language of the church in America.

In the next year, Archbishop Innokenty was consecrated as Metropolitan of Moscow, the highest position in the Russian Orthodox church, which he held until his death. While in Moscow he never forgot his flock in America; in 1870 he established the Russian Imperial Missionary Society, which provided necessary funds to support the newly created American diocese, the Diocese of Alaska and the Aleutian Islands. In 1977 he was canonized a saint by the Russian Orthodox Church with the designation "Saint Innokenty of Moscow, Enlightener of the Aleuts and Apostle to America." He died in Moscow on March 31, 1879.

Papers relating to Saint Innokenty are in the Alaskan Russian Church Archives, Library of Congress, which published a catalog in 1984, and in the Territorial Library, Juneau, Alaska. For additional biographical information see Paul D. Garrett, *St. Innocent, Apostle to America* (1979), and Lev Puhalo, *Innokenty of Alaska* (1976). His work is also discussed in Michael Oleksa, ed., *Alaskan Missionary Spirituality* (1987), and Constance J. Tarasar, ed., Orthodox America, 1794-1976 (1975).

David C. Ford, reprinted with the gracious permission of Oxford University Press)

Ioann (Stephan Mitropolsky)

Bishop of the Aleutians, he graduated from the Moscow Theological Academy and in 1870 was appointed bishop. In 1881 he became the Abbot of the Moscow Simonov Monastery and in 1889 he was made bishop of Aksa.

Konstantin Konstantinovich (1858-1915)

Grand Duke and second son of Konstantin Nikolaevich, he was the President of the Academy of Science and also a poet.

Konstantin Nikolaevich (1827-1892)

Grand Duke and second son of Nicholas I, he was brother and a close associate of Alexander II. He was a man of liberal views and instituted many reforms. Nicholas I wanted his son to serve in the Navy. In 1855 Konstantin Nikolaevich assumed the command of the Navy and the Department of the Navy. Under his leadership the Russian Navy was streamlined; for instance, he replaced vessels having sails with engine ships and abolished corporal punishment. He also attracted many Russian intellectuals, including authors and writers, to his domain of naval activity. Among them was the famous Russian writer Goncharov, who served as a secretary in the Putiatin diplomatic mission. Konstantin Nikolaevich also tried to protect the interests of Russian peasants. In 1865 he was appointed chairman of the State Council. He was a key figure in the process of selling Alaska and contributed to a closer relationship between Russia and the United States. When Alexander II died he retired from politics and lived a quiet life.

Konstantin Pavlovich (1779-1831)

Grand Duke and second son of Paul I, he was raised under the supervision of Catherine II. During the enthusiasm caused by the Potemkin Greek Project she had in mind to put her grandson on the throne of the future Byzantine (Constantinople) Empire to be revived after the Turks were driven out of Europe. Konstantin fought in the war with Napoleon and was a commander of the Guards. He was a shareholder of the Russian-American Company.

Kruzenstern, Ivan Fedorovich (1770-1846)

Admiral and the first Russian to lead an around the world voyage of the ships *Nadezhda* and *Neva* (1803-1806). He was a member of various Academies of Science in Europe. He was also a member of the American Philosophy Society.

Lisiansky, Yuri Fedorovich (1773-1837)

A seafarer and captain, he was sent by Catherine II to serve in the British Navy. He made several voyages to North America and for some time lived in Philadelphia, where he was invited to many American homes. At the request of the Russian-American Company he purchased ships in America. During the first Russian voyage around the world he was the captain of the *Neva*. His book, *Voyage around the world in 1803, 1804, 1805 and 1806* was published in 1812 and translated into English.

Maria Fedorovna (1759-1828)

Born German Princess Sophia Dorothea Augusta Louise, she became the wife of Paul I. Catherine II kept her away from raising her sons Alexander and Konstantin taking them from her immediately after their birth. After Paul ascended the throne she became actively involved in charity and the education of young people, especially young women. She was a shareholder of the Russian-American Company.

Maria Fedorovna (1847-1928)

Born Danish Princess Maria, Sophia, Frederica, Dagmar, she was the daughter of the Danish King Christian IX. In 1886 she married Alexander Alexandrovich, a son of Alexander II, who later became Alexander III. During the visit of the American ship *Monatonomo* in Europe, she visited the ship with the royal family. Maria Fedorovna was well loved by the Russian people and the army. During the revolution in Russia in 1917 she demonstrated outstanding courage.

Nicholas I (1796-1855)

He was the third son of Paul I and became Emperor of Russia in 1825. He had not been involved in state affairs before ascending the throne because his elder brother was to be successor to the throne. Since childhood he enjoyed military games. He was a division commander before becoming ruler. During his rule Russia was involved in major wars in the Caucasus, fighting against Persia and Turkey. During the Crimean war of 1853-1856 a coalition of European powers joined Turkey against Russia. Only the United States of America demonstrated sympathy and declared neutrality. Severe stress and strain caused by the war affected his good health and Nicholas died before the war was over.

His reign was marked by an effort to present Russia as a special state. In his view, Russia should be distinct from the rest of Europe in all aspects of state and national life as there was only one way for Russia to be organized.

Michael Pavlovich (1798-1848)

Grand Duke and fourth son of Paul I, he had been interested in everything involving the military since childhood. He fought in many wars and had an abundance of military awards. Michael Pavlovich distinguished himself as an officer devoted to military service who expected high performance both from himself and his subordinates. He was a shareholder of the Russian- American Company.

Paul I (1754-1801)

He became Russian Emperor in 1796. As a child he grew apart from his mother as Empress Elizabeth, daughter of Peter I, took him away from his family and raised him herself. Irreconcilable differences developed between him and his mother (Catherine II). When Paul came to the throne at the age of 42 he had already become an irritable and wretched person. He made an enormous effort to change all the procedures introduced by Catherine II. But he lacked the talents of a statesman and his mother's vision. The five-year reign of Paul I displeased all of Russian society. He exiled his wife and sons, alienating them from court. A group of noblemen led by the military governor of Petersburg staged a palace coup and as a result Paul I was assassinated and Alexander I was put on the throne.

Peter I (1672-1725)

He became Tsar in 1682 at the age of four. His elder brother and stepsister Princess Sofia were his regents. As a child and young adult he lived in a highly disturbing and tumultuous time for Russia and all of these influences greatly affected him. His reign as sole ruler began in 1689 signifying a time of unprecedented reforms in Russia. Changes were introduced in almost all aspects of Russian life.

Potemkin, Gregory Alexandrovich (1739-1791)

Prince, General-Field Marshal and famous favorite of Catherine II, he attended Moscow University and together with other elite students was introduced to Empress

Elizabeth Petrovna, daughter of Peter I. Later, however, he became lazy and was expelled from the University for "poor attendance." He owed his incredible career to his participation in the palace coup and Catherine's favors. He advised Catherine on most important state documents. One of his foremost accomplishments was the establishment of a Russian fleet in the Black Sea and the annexation of the Crimea. In 1787 he arranged Catherine's famous journey to the south of Russia, which resulted in triumph. People's opinions of Potemkin while he was alive and after he died were as different as black and white. Some people called him the Empress's evil wizard and a prince of darkness, while others, including Catherine herself, thought that he was a man of genius. One thing is clear; he was one of the greatest celebrities of the age of Catherine the Great.

Putiatin, Efim Vasilievich (1803-1883)

Count, diplomat, admiral, and Minister of Education, he was a great connoisseur of nautical travel, a man full of determination who did not lose his presence of mind in the most dangerous situations. He made his first 5-year voyage to the northwestern coast of America. He was highly successful in accomplishing various diplomatic missions on behalf of the Russian Government, particularly in his mission to Japan for which he received an Imperial Gramota and the title of Count. He supported the idea of strengthening Russian influence in South East Asia, stood for cooperation with the United States and was in favor of selling Alaska to the US.

Philaret (Vasily Mikhailovich Drozdov) (1783-1867)

Metropolitan of Moscow, he was a graduate of the Seminary of the Trinity-St. Sergius Monastery. In 1868 he took monastic vows. In 1821 he was an archbishop of the

Moscow diocese and the archimandrite of the Trinity–St. Sergius Monastery. He was made Metropolitan in 1826. He focused special attention on the development of religious schools and seminaries, on spiritual and moral enlightenment and was involved in many diverse charities. He was a great preacher and his sermons were translated into French and German. He translated the Gospels into Russian and wrote the Manifesto on the Abolition of Serfdom, dated February 19, 1861. Alexander II greatly respected him.

Metropolitan Philaret was also very interested in the outstanding missionary work of Fr. Ivan Veniaminov, who later succeeded him as Metropolitan of Moscow, Innokenty. Philaret greatly supported his efforts in Alaska and the two became great friends. Metropolitan Philaret was canonized by the Russian Orthodox Church in 1994.

Rezanov, Nicholas Petrovich (1764-1807)

Government official Court Chamberlain, Ambassador to Japan, and a founder of the Russian-American Company, he was born in St. Petersburg on 28 March 1764, the son of Petr Gavrilovich Rezanov, a judge. After receiving primary education at home, in 1778, at age 14, Rezanov entered the artillery and then, through some influence was enrolled in the prestigious Izmailovskii guards regiment in St. Petersburg, He evidently was unsuited for military life, for in the 1780s, after only about two years, for reasons unknown, he left the service and became assessor in the Civil Court Chamber at Pskov, a minor position in a provincial town. Five years later he transferred to the Treasury Office (Kazennaia Palata), another ordinary position, but in St. Petersburg. In 1787, after two years in that capacity, he became chief clerk in the office of Count I.G. Chernyshev, Vice President and later Executor of the Admiralty College. In 1781, upon appointment of G.R. Derzhavin (1743-1816), poet and courtier and family friend of the

Rezanovs for two decades, as Secretary for Senate Reports, Rezanov was appointed Chief Clerk of Derzhavin's office. Thus after a succession of ordinary jobs he had now achieved entry into the court. For a while he even served on the staff of the Empress' favorite, Prince P.A. Zubov, and was employed by the Empress for special assignments. Thus he was assigned to compile a statute on workshops, and to establish apportionment of the land tax in St. Petersburg and Moscow. For the latter work he was awarded the Order of St. Anna 2nd degree, and a pension of 2,000 rubles a year.

Around 1794 or 1795, Rezanov was sent on some mission to Irkutsk, where his father still served in the courts. There he became acquainted - or renewed earlier acquaintance - with G.I. Shelikhov, listened eagerly to the latter's plans for the fur trade in the Pacific, and married his daughter, Anna. Rezanov was not a count or baron, i.e., of the titled nobility, but his position made him one of the lesser nobility. Therefore her status as the daughter of a merchant would have made the marriage something of a mesalliance had it not been for Shelikhov's prominence and prospects. Rezanov's connection with Zubov was valuable for him and for his father-in-law, and it was probably at Shelikhov's behest, inspired by hope and influencing the Empress, that Rezanov engineered the naming of the islands discovered by Pribylov in 1786 the Zubov Islands.

Upon Shelikhov's death, 20 July 1795, Rezanov became protector of the family interests, and after the death of the Empress Catherine, on 6 November 1796, his power grew through new rank and privileges obtained under Catherine's son and successor, the Emperor Paul In 1791 he was assigned to the Senate as Secretary, and a month later was made Chief Secretary.

Catherine II had opposed monopolies throughout her reign, but under Paul I there was hope of a reversal of this stand,

and Rezanov worked hard behind the scenes to bring this about. On 11 August 1799, Rezanov obtained an Imperial ukaz sanctioning formation of the Russian--American Company.

When the Emperor Alexander I came to the throne, 12 March 1801, his remorse over the death of his father may have caused him to give special favor to those who had served under Paul. Thus Rezanov was made a member of the Finland Commission. At his urging, the Emperor and many members of the Imperial house became shareholders in the Russian-American Company, as well as many members of St. Petersburg society and merchants. By the end of 1801 the number of shareholders had risen from 17 to 400.

About 18 July 1801, Rezanov's wife, Anna Grigor'evna, bore him a son, Petr. On 6 October 1802, she bore a daughter, Ol'ga, but died twelve days later. For Rezanov, grief-stricken, a welcome diversion appeared in a projected voyage around the world to the American colonies. Supply for the colonies was a constant problem, so for cheaper and safer transport, especially of heavier items, he and others had urged the use of sea transport, an idea already proposed in the 1780s. At his urging, the RAC purchased two trading vessels in England, renamed the *Neva* and *Nadezhda*, to be under Iu.F.Lisianskii and I.F. Kruzenstern. The *Neva* would go to Russian America, and the *Nadezhda* to Kamchatka. Only a month before the ships were to sail, on 10 June 1803, Rezanov received the Order of St. Anna 1st degree and the title of Chamberlain of the Imperial Court, and was assigned to the expedition to sail on the *Nadezhda*.

On 16 July 1803 the two vessels left Kronshtadt. During the voyage, Rezanov and Kruzenstern were at odds over who was in command, a conflict taken up avidly by Kruzenstern's junior officers, who so plagued the ambassador with taunts, practical jokes and even threats on his life, that

Rezanov finally retired to his cabin where he stayed until the ship reached Kamchatka. There an enquiry conducted by the commandant, Major General Koshelev, placed Kruzenstern in such a bad light that to save his career he publicly begged Rezanov's pardon, and sent the latter's chief tormenter, Lieutenant Count Tolstoi, back to St. Petersburg.

From Petropavlovsk, Kamchatka, Rezanov and his physician G.A. Langsdorf took the RAC vessel *Sv. Maria Magdalena* to America. Stopping briefly at the Pribylovs, Unalashka and Kad'iak, they arrived in Novo-Arkhangel'sk (Sitka) on 26 August, where the chief manager, Baranov, was directing the building of a fort. Soon coming to admire Baranov, Rezanov observed company affairs, and in long reports to the company and to the Emperor made many recommendations. The American vessel *Juno*, of 250 tons, had arrived 14 August, and her captain, John D'Wolf, was willing to sell. Baranov and Rezanov concluded the bargain and sent the ship under Lieutenants Khvostov and Davydov to Kad'iak for a cargo of dried fish.

In 1806 in order to obtain supplies with which to allay the continuing food shortage, Rezanov sent the *Juno* to San Francisco, himself going as a passenger. There by slyness and charm he gained universal approval from the Spanish administrators, the mission fathers, and the general population. The celebrated betrothal with Concepcion Arguello, the 16 year-old daughter of the commandant, helped him obtain the desired cargo of foodstuffs. Under the pretext of searching for allegedly fugitive seamen, he ordered his men to reconnoiter the north shore of San Francisco Bay, gaining knowledge of the terrain later useful in making plans for establishment of the Ross settlement and fort a few miles up the coast.

Returning to Sitka, Rezanov took the next ship to Okhotsk. From there he started across Siberia, at break-neck speed. On the way, however, he contracted a fever, and in March 1807 died at Krasnoyarsk.

Rezanov was buried near the old Krasnoyarsk cathedral. Langsdorf, who went through Krasnoyarsk the following November, observed a large stone over the grave as a temporary monument. In 1831, a quarter of a century later, the RAC erected a granite monolith over the spot, where it existed until both cathedral and monument were razed in 1935 to make way for new construction.

A dreamer with ambition, Rezanov sought a prosperous, strong Russian establishment in North America. He urged repeatedly that Russian settlements be placed at the mouth of the Columbia River and down the coast as far as Spanish California. He wanted to freeze out American competition in the fur trade, thereby enhancing Russian profits and depriving the inhabitants of the liquor and firearms which caused disorder and threatened the Russian settlements. He urged conservation of fur-bearing animals by closed seasons on hunting, instead of the wasteful methods then in use. He recommended that the hunters be paid a fixed salary instead of by shares of the catch, insuring a steady income (a reform not introduced until 1818). His plans, extending those of Shelikhov, could have given Russia a firm foothold on the Pacific Coast, and a share in Pacific trade. However, the government had more pressing concerns elsewhere, and in spite of A.A. Baranov's efforts, the wider plans remained unachieved. N.P. Rezanov's own name appears on the map of Alaska only in Rezanof Lake, on south central Baranof Island, so designated in 1933 by the U.S. Forest Service. There is also a Rezanov Street in Kodiak, and another in Anchorage.

From Richard A. Pierce, *Russian America: A Biographical Dictionary*, reprinted with the gracious permission of The Limestone Press.

Shelikhov, Gregory Ivanovich (1747-1795)

Merchant, founder of the first permanent Russian settlement in Alaska. (Others in his family spell the name Shelekhov). He was born in 1748, in the small southern Russian trading center of Ryl'sk, in Kursk gubernia, of a family of merchants. Nothing is known of his youth, but it is clear that he acquired a modest education and learned business methods. In 1772, at about 25 years of age, he went to Siberia, and by 1773 was a prikashchik or agent of Ivan Larionovich Golikov (1729-1805), a merchant of Kursk who had settled in Irkutsk. In 1775, Shelikhov married. His bride, Natal'ia Alekseevna Shelikhov (original surname unknown), was probably the daughter or widow of some rich merchant, and thus an initial source of Shelikhov's capital.

In 1774, Shelikhov went to Iakutsk, two thousand versts northward, down the Lena River, and from there another thousand versts overland to Okhotsk, where he began to take part in companies backing fur trading voyages to the Kurile Islands and the Aleutians. In eight years he participated in at least ten companies. In 1779 Shelikhov proposed that one company be given a monopoly over the trade throughout the islands and the American mainland.

In Irkutsk, Shelikhov obtained permission to build ships and authorization to take needed goods and supplies from government stores. He hired workmen, and transported them and needed materials to Okhotsk. He was backed in part by N. Demidov, a Ural mining magnate, who loaned him 50,000 rubles. At the mouth of the river Urak, near Okhotsk, Shelikhov and the two Golikovs built three galiots, the *Tri Sviatitelia* (Three Hierarchs), the *Sv. Semen* (St. Simeon), and the *Sv. Mikhail* (St. Michael).

The expedition sailed on 16 August. On board the vessels were 192 officers and men, including Shelikhov himself, his wife and their two children, several relatives, and his partner, Captain M.S. Golikov.

On 13 July 1784 they arrived at Unalashka. After obtaining fresh water and making repairs they put to sea again on 22 July. Shelikhov took along two Fox Island Aleuts as interpreters - he calls them "volunteers" - and two as workers.

On 3 August the two vessels reached the island of Kykhtak, or as it became know, Kad'iak (Kodiak).

The first winter, of 1784-1785, was hard, with several deaths from scurvy. In the spring, he sent out parties to reconnoiter and obtain furs. The second winter, of 1785-1786, was easier, with improved shelter and a better food supply.

By the spring of 1786, more supplies and reinforcements were needed, so Shelikhov prepared to return to Okhotsk with the *Tri Sviatitelia*. He and his wife left Okhotsk by dog team on 8 February 1787, reaching Iakutsk 11 March, and Irkutsk on 6 April.

In Irkutsk, Shelikhov reported to Governor-General Iakobii, submitting lengthy written accounts (one of which became the basis for his well-known book, published in 1791), maps, plans for a great monopoly, and requests for a hundred men trained in arms, specialists, and two priests and a deacon. He asked permission to carry on further trade with the English, and held out the hope of profitable future trade relations with Japan, Korea, China and India, the Philippine Islands, and the Spanish and the Americans (Indians) in America. He asked that the company be allowed to establish enterprises on any island it should discover, bringing them under the Russian scepter. He asked for a loan of 500,000 rubles for twenty years, and the loan of one of the government ships at Okhotsk. Iakobii approved Shelikhov's proposals and lauded his measures for conversion and education of the natives.

About December 1788, Shelikhov, his wife, and Golikov left for St. Petersburg to report to the government about his voyage and plans, and to seek sanction for his requests. In February 1789, he and Golikov submitted a petition to the Empress reviewing Shelikhov's exploits and outlining future plans, stressing their love of country and zeal for the public welfare, and presenting a scaled-down request for 200,000 rubles.

The time for such a request seemed right, as in July 1785 the Empress authorized the extensive expedition of Captain Joseph Billings, and in 1787 authorized Captain G. Mulovskii to sail around the world with four ships into the North Pacific. However, the Empress was a convinced free trader, and in 1788 the country was at war with Turkey and Sweden, and had neither money nor soldiers to spare. In the end Catherine approved only an award of gold medals and silver sabers to Shelikhov and Golikov, and a citation lauding them for their achievements.

Shelikhov left the capital for Irkutsk, probably none too soon, as on 2 November, Captain Billings forwarded the complaints of a surgeon's assistant, Miron Britiukov, who had sailed to America with Shelikhov on the *Tri Sviatitelia*, concerning Shelikhov's abuse of the natives of the islands of Kad'iak, Shuiakh and Afognak. Britiukov's accusations were quashed by the Okhotsk authorities, but they besmirched Shelikhov's reputation.

Shelikhov then passed the winter of 1789-1790 in Irkutsk, where he made new efforts to obtain government aid. Governor-General Iakobii was replaced by Ivan Alfer'evich Pil, and Shelikhov was successful in enlisting his support. Seeking a new manager in America Shelikhov was able to enlist Aleksandr Andreevich Baranov, a merchant from Kargopol, and a veteran of Siberian trade. The two concluded a contract on 10 August 1790 and on 18 August Baranov sailed on the *Tri Sviatitelia*. He would remain in the colonies for the next 28 years, his selection perhaps Shelikhov's greatest achievement.

Shelikhov's request for clergy for the colonies bore fruit when, in an ukaz of 30 June 1793, the Empress ordered a group of missionaries to be sent. His request for colonists was granted by an ukaz of 31 December 1793. In the summer of 1794, 52 craftsmen and peasants and their families, and 10 clergymen, the latter led by the Archimandrite Ioasaf, were assembled at Okhotsk and sent to Kad'iak on the *Tri Sviatitelia* and the *Sv. Ekaterina*

Then, suddenly, in Irkutsk, on 20 July 1795, Shelikhov died. The cause of his death remains uncertain. The symptoms indicate some intestinal complaint.

Catherine II died soon thereafter in 1796. Under the new sovereign, Paul I, other merchants tried to wrest control of the company from Natal'ia Shelikhov, and the Emperor, disgusted by reports of abuses against the natives of the Aleutian Islands, was about to abolish the company's privileges. However, Natal'ia's determination, and the efforts of her highly placed son-in-law, N.P. Rezanov, saved the day. Rezanov, whose wife's inheritance consisted mainly of company shares, worked hard behind the scenes, and was able to swing Paul over to the idea of a monopoly. By a decree of 8 July, 1799 the Russian-American Company was formed. Built on the foundation laid by Shelikhov, it was destined to survive for nearly 70 years.

From Richard A. Pierce, *Russian America: A Biographical Dictionary*, reprinted with the gracious permission of The Limestone Press)

Trinity-St. Sergius Monastery

One of the most ancient and venerated monasteries in Russia, it was founded by St. Sergius of Radonezh in the middle of the 14th century. The monastery played an important role in Russia's political and religious affairs, and it has always been under the special patronage of Russian tsars and emperors. In 1742 a seminary was established, which was affiliated with the monastery. Visiting the monastery was a necessity for Russians and foreign guests, especially at the time of coronations and official celebrations. The monastery was a center of Orthodox religious pilgrimages and it was there that Metropolitan Filaret received the American, Mr. Fox.

N.A. Kargapolova
M.P. Swezey